929.6

D0240386

THE
HERALDIC ART
SOURCE BOOK

THE
HERALDIC ART
SOURCE BOOK

Peter Spurrier

BLANDFORD

A BLANDFORD BOOK

First published in the UK 1997 by Blandford
A Cassell Imprint
Cassell Plc, Wellington House,
125 Strand, London WC2R 0BB

Distributed in the United States by Sterling Publishing Co., Inc.,
387 Park Avenue South, New York, NY 10016–8810

**A Cataloguing-in-Publication Data entry for this title is available
from the British Library**

ISBN 0 7137 2708 X

Typeset by Business ColorPrint, Welshpool, Powys, Wales

Printed and bound in Great Britain by Bath Press, Bath

CONTENTS

FOREWORD

Although interest in heraldry has vastly increased over the
past half-century – witness the number of local heraldry
societies which have grown apace and the ever increasing
volume of books on many aspects of the subject –
I cannot bring to mind a book on basic heraldry
written by a practising, professional heraldic artist and
certainly not by one who himself was once a herald.
This alone gives this book a special flavour, not previously
tasted, and it is one that is most agreeable.

Peter Spurrier's illustrations are an exciting adjunct to the
text, or is it the other way round? Certainly they
complement each other, coming together to make a singular
and useful addition to anyone's heraldic library.

Of particular interest is the chapter on monsters.
The late Rodney Denny's book, *The Heraldic Imagination*,
has excited interest in this aspect of heraldry, which
has an appeal far beyond the confines of armory and
it is a pleasure to see so many curiosities detailed
and so vividly depicted in a book on heraldry, rather
than in a beastiary.

Heraldry used to be and many still regard it as
an exact science. Artists know better and although there
are rules, there is more than a little artistic latitude in
their observance. Peter Spurrier has highlighted this
important aspect of what we are pleased to call 'the Art
and Science of Heraldry'.

John Brooke-Little
Clarenceux King of Arms

INTRODUCTION

WHILE several excellent books have been published on the history and development of heraldic design, none seem to encompass the entire spectrum of decorative techniques from the earliest times to the present day.

It would be comparatively simple to write a studio 'workshop manual' or a do-it-yourself book on the subject but as with many other disciplines, any real progress in one's work is only achieved through practical experience. It is my intention therefore in this book not only to provide ample material for the armchair craftsman and the Sunday painter to browse upon, but also to include solid practical advice and evidence based upon some years of hard experience.

With the demise of heraldic drawing in art schools a valuable means of training future designers in the basic rudiments of shape, form and colour has been lost, for surely heraldry requires practised skills in the field of still life, figure and animal anatomy, arms and armour, fruit and vegetables, foliage, all portrayed within a given shape or area.

Scientific work has been undertaken in recent years to examine the safest and clearest combination of colours to use on motorways, in factories and at sea. The results confirm the system that was largely devised by heraldic painters towards the end of the twelfth century. A colour placed upon another colour will not show up well at a distance, neither will a metal show up well on another metal. Even the old adage 'blue and green should not be seen, without a colour in between' still holds good. I am sure the early heraldic painters would have used fluorescent colours had they been available.

We pretend today to be so advanced, but in reality much design work is turning full circle. The modern motor-racing safety helmet, with its rear wall cut away above the nape of the neck to prevent injury, is much more like the ancient pot-helm than many intervening designs. Why should this be?

Is it through ignorance, fashion or just a lack of interest in creating new designs? Too often we placidly accept the uninspired instructions of uninspired teachers. I am glad to see that as we take more heed of our past, the early spirit of invention is returning to the drawing-boards and benches of young designers and a bold new style is gradually emerging in the graphic and plastic arts.

As important as art school training is, it should not attempt to provide the answers but rather to make the problems and difficulties abundantly clear. Then, if we have the means of clear thinking and design analysis, with hard work and a little inspiration, reasonable solutions should be found.

The increasing popularity of heraldry as a hobby is especially encouraging with new groups of enthusiasts getting together all over the country. Thirty years ago there was just one major society for amateur heraldists, The Heraldry Society, based in London, and one other small group in the North of England. Now there are dozens of small local societies catering for the amateur heraldist by providing lecture programmes and outings to places of heraldic interest, thus fulfilling a social need in rural areas. More people are taking up heraldically motivated hobbies such as glass-engraving, painting on vellum and wood-carving. The Society of Heraldic Arts was founded in 1987 essentially for professional craftsmen and women.

Modern heraldic artists are fortunate to have the amazing range of colourings that are now available in artists' supply shops – oil colours, water colours, gouache, acrylics, enamels and so on, together with a vast variety of materials to paint and draw upon. It is interesting however that for special jobs, the old materials are always requested – vellum, hand-ground colour, raised gold-leaf on hand-prepared gesso and water strained paper. It is of course known that the old materials have stood the test of time and it may well be that aluminium leaf will not turn black in 300 years' time and fibreglass will mature beautifully.

It is interesting to note how aware film and television companies now are of heraldic niceties with particular attention being paid to accuracy in period productions. With the growing interest in heraldry, television companies must be pestered with complaints at the smallest errors on the screen. Everyone likes to show that they know better! Another aspect of the popular usage of heraldry is its role in interior design, for example in Tudor-Elizabethan-style dining-rooms in restaurants and hotels where authenticity is now expected, which of course provides work for the interior decorator with an interest in heraldic art.

I am sometimes asked why exactly people like discreet heraldic display. Why are cufflinks and signet rings engraved with a family crest these days when sealing wax is not much used? Why is the best table silver engraved with armorial ensigns when it is unlikely that our friends will steal the spoons? Why do some cars have crests on the doors? It is easy to understand why schools, universities and clubs use heraldic devices on their effects for visual identification at gatherings where many students or members are involved, but the personal use of arms and crests these days is more complicated. Putting aside any snobbish feelings of superiority, which may or may not play some part, I think that some people are looking for individuality within an organized system. In the same way that women's clothes must conform to the requirements of warmth and modesty, but be distinctive, a coat of arms must conform to the basic rules and yet it must be unique. In this way an armigerous person is distinctive, and if the device has been passed down through the family, so much the better. Nevertheless, a brand new grant of arms has all the qualities of an old one except the dignity of age.

People have often asked me if it is difficult to think up and design new coats of arms continually and my answer is that there are only so many notes on the piano keyboard but composers are still writing new music.

Peter Spurrier

THE HISTORY AND ORIGINS OF HERALDRY

IT is generally agreed that heraldry as an organized system emerged in Europe at the end of the twelfth century. It seems that there was an almost simultaneous blooming of banners and shields in both England and on the Continent without any tangible reason or connection. It was as if someone had fired a starting gun and shouted, 'Heraldry now exists'.

If we examine the Bayeux tapestry, we can see that the pennons at the soldiers' lance points are decorated in a haphazard way and with no apparent system, and the flags on the ships are no better than wind vanes. Indeed Duke William used a lantern and a horn for signalling purposes rather than flags. Heraldry was born of necessity in handling and organizing large numbers of illiterate men not only on the battlefield but in camp before and after engagements. The army, messengers and itinerants such as minstrels and troubadors were the only people to travel much at that time, and it would have been the British army commanders who adopted what was probably a European invention, namely a simple means of visual identification. The idea worked so well that a system soon developed in England although slightly different to the one used on the Continent.

The catalyst in the development was the feudal system which required every baron and landholder to provide a given number of knights and foot-soldiers to serve their king and country on the battlefield when required. In return the barons had grants of land and other perquisites. This meant that at any large gathering there would be numerous barons acting as 'team-leaders', each with his own company of mounted men and infantry which could amount to hundreds of men and horses. The only way to identify any such group before the introduction of uniforms and regimental badges, was by means of a system of flags and banners. This was the obvious way of marking a group and identifying the leader so that in a crowded place one could see in which direction he was going, in much the

Fig. 1   Sir Robert de Setvans (1306)

same way as guides in London today hold an umbrella with a handkerchief tied to the top aloft for the benefit of their parties of tourists.

I suspect that heraldic marks were used at first on flags rather than on shields. If the leader in battle was where he should be, advancing at the head of his troops, it was only the enemy who could see the device on his shield and not his loyal men following him. I feel certain that each company commander was accompanied by a standard-bearer or a banner-man, which honourable office may well have suggested this soldier's surname or appelation.

It is not clear how devices were chosen initially, and it must be assumed that shapes and marks were adopted at random so long as they were distinctive. A popular theory is that the partition lines in heraldry, such as 'bends', 'bars' and 'chevrons', represent the timber construction of the shield, but surely the framework of the shield would be at the back and obscured by the soldier's body. The front of the shield would be smooth and inviting decoration.

When heraldry was in its infancy, the designs were simple and easy to recognize, but with the passing years, many of the basic devices were used and cannot be used again. Therefore the designs became more complicated and more monsters appeared which were either drawn from existing bestiaries or created by the heraldic artist. For example, a griffin has an eagle's head with ears, talons and wings on the body of a lion (see *Plate XIV*). This creature is generally shown with male attributes, but there is another monster known as a male griffin (see *Plate XII*) which has no wings, has tufts or spikes issuing from its head and body and is also shown with male attributes. There seems to be no such creature as a female griffin. The tufts on the male griffin must surely represent bunches of feathers blown out by the wind, as seen when the griffin-vulture is sunning itself. This is possibly a dim memory from crusading days.

The only people likely to have seen a lion or a vulture would have been crusading knights. Upon returning to their English village months or even years later, a verbal description would be the only guide to their local scribe or to the cart-painter, as these gallant artists wrestled with what they considered mythical beasts. After the baron or knight had returned home from a military campaign with his men, all of whom would probably have been agricultural labourers, and normal village life resumed, his shield and banner would have been put in some prominent place for all to see and admire the scars of war. Many churches and chapels today display battle-soiled flags and colours in honour and memory of past glories. So the device on the shield and on the flag would become well known to the villagers who would regard it as their own village badge. When a knight died, his son would continue to use the device rather than confusing his tenant villagers by adopting a different one. In this way the whole idea of an hereditary system fell into step with titles, surnames and privileges.

It was perfectly natural therefore that coat armour, or coats of arms, should become part of the trappings of the knightly classes. As heraldry developed, a knight would have his arms embroidered on to a surcoat which he wore over his armour giving rise to the expression coat armour. The memorial brass to Sir Robert de Setvans in the church at Chartham in Kent shows this (*Fig. 1*). In due course the use of the knight's heraldic device was extended to cover many of his personal effects and in this way they were both identified and beautified. Craftsmen of all disciplines studied the rules and the use of heraldry; the illustrations in this book bear testament to the wide range of skills that converted a means of military identification into an art-form.

It is sad that examples of very early flags have not survived in the same way that metal-work and ceramics have done. The earliest heraldic fabric is found in the beautifully worked copes worn by the clergy, so it is difficult to prove whether or not the use of devices on flags occurred before shields. Manuscript illustrations are the main source of information and although they sometimes fault the armour, there are always plenty of banners on show.

Between 1530 and 1690 the heralds travelled throughout England to check that coats of arms were being used with lawful authority. It was every gentleman's duty to appear before the heralds and cite the provenance of his armorial bearing. These were recorded in books which were lodged at the College of Arms and are still in daily use for research purposes.

For those people not entitled to bear arms and unwilling to do so without lawful authority, the alternative was a rebus. This was a picture or a figure representing a word or name visually. A rebus was not registered or recorded officially and it could be used by artisans and craftsmen at will, although this method of visual identification was also often adopted by persons of rank who had no claim to arms. The two examples shown here were those used by John Islip, Abbot of Westminster (*Fig. 2*), and Thomas Beckynton, Bishop of Bath and Wells, 1443–65 (*Fig. 3*), both men of the

Fig. 2   The rebus ('I slip') of John Islip

Fig. 3   The rebus ('Beacon-tun') of Thomas Beckynton

church who might have considered a coat of arms would appear too military or be an act of self-aggrandisement. The former rebus can be seen in the Abbot's chantry chapel and the latter in the Rector's lodgings at Lincoln College, Oxford. For a rebus to be successful it must be self-explanatory as a visual pun upon a name. To understand these two illustrations, one must know that a 'slip' is a branch or a plant stem pulled off the main trunk, and that a 'tun' means a barrel in heraldry.

Like the oar-maces of the Admiralty and the maces of the City livery companies, the heralds' wands indicate not authority but that a legal or ceremonial occasion is in session. It is believed that the wands were originally used to support lengthy documents which were being read out in the open air. The officers of arms have two kinds of wand which they carry at the State Opening of Parliament and at the annual Garter service at Windsor Castle. The older wands have a black shaft headed with the badge of their office in gilt but these were thought to be too sombre for the Queen's coronation in 1953, so new wands were made with white shafts tipped with the crest of the College of Arms, namely a white dove rising from a gold coronet.

HERALDRY TODAY

THERE are a number of reasons why people today should want either to display their inherited arms or to apply to the Kings of Arms for a brand new coat of arms. If arms have been inherited, there must be a quiet sense of pride that the bearer's family has been established for some years. This must give a feeling of confidence in our modern times when so many traditional values have been overturned. Other people may wish to make a small but indelible mark in the heraldic records by applying for their own new arms. All shields were new at some time and a grant of arms with the ink still wet is just as honourable as the oldest, and will be in the official records for as long as the College of Arms exists. Some applicants for new arms have fostered a genuine love of history and chivalry all their lives and wish to be part of it, while a very few yearn for a shield and crest to be granted to them so that they can consider themselves to be on a higher social level than their friends. According to the books of precedent, a man is a 'gentleman' only if he is entitled to armorial bearings.

In heraldry, females bear the arms of their father until they marry. If they marry a man who is entitled to arms, they may impale their paternal arms with those of their husband. Until recently if the husband was not entitled to arms, the wife could not retain hers. Under a new ruling, however, from the Kings of Arms, wives of non-armigerous men may continue to bear the arms of their father.

If a female has no brothers and her father is entitled to arms, she is an heraldic heiress and places her paternal shield 'in pretence' in the centre of her husband's shield. After their demise, their children will quarter their parent's arms.

Females display their paternal arms on lozenges and not on shields as of course they did not use these. Nor do they use crests as they did not wear helmets.

The question of why people want armorial bearings has to be addressed every day by the heralds at the College of Arms. Over 200 new grants of arms are made each year by virtue of a warrant from the Duke of Norfolk in his capacity as Earl Marshal and Marshal of England. The Earl Marshal acts as the sovereign's lieutenant in matters armorial and provides the authority for the Kings of Arms to grant arms, which are by nature hereditary honours from the Crown.

Fig. 4   The Prince of Wales's feathers

Why do people in the twentieth century still want an outmoded means of personal identification? The answer is, I believe, nothing to do with snobbishness, but that in this transitory life with its professional stress and domestic pressure, people are still looking for ways of laying down a solid foundation for their family. Heraldry is traditional; it is also fun, colourful, historic and respected. Furthermore, it was out of the reach of many until the present generation. Social mobility and substantial financial rewards have opened up the whole field of armory and genealogy to people who two or three generations ago would not, or could not, contemplate the prospect of a grant of arms. So who does qualify?

A grant of arms is a gesture of recognition from the Crown and is the only honour that can properly be applied for. The fees paid to the Crown do not represent the cost of the grant, which is made on merit, but help to support the College of Arms which has been the repository of armorial documents for over 500 years. The basic qualification for a petitioner, or applicant for a grant of armorial bearings, is that he or she (and arms have always been granted to women) is a person of good standing and has contributed to society by having some role in the community. This may be in any field of public service from the Scout movement to the government, but some evidence of contribution is essential if the Kings of Arms are to look favourably upon an applicant. It is certainly also helpful if the petitioner has achieved success in their career and possibly holds a university degree or professional qualifications. A commission in the armed services also helps to establish whether a person is of sufficient standing to support the honour of a grant of arms and the rank of gentleman or gentlewoman. The over-riding fact is that armorial bearings cannot be bought, like the lordship of a manor which may be ancient and eminently respectable, but is not in the nature of an honour.

DESCRIPTION OF A COAT OF ARMS

THE most efficient way to describe a coat of arms is to use the heralds' language or technical jargon, known as blazon. This is a simple and straightforward method of expressing the design and colours of arms and crests, yet allowing a certain degree of flexibility for the artist in the graphic interpretation. It does not really take long to master the basics of the heraldic system with the assistance of a beginner's book of heraldry, and it is great fun to work out some of the really complicated designs and describe them in the correct technical terms. The general layout of a coat of arms is shown in *Fig. 5*.

The colour, or tincture, of the shield should always be given first, followed by the items contained in the design. Heraldic colours are clear and bright and no exact specification has ever been laid down regarding hues, although some manufacturers, particularly in the flag-making industry, insist upon a British Standard number to avoid misunderstanding. Items shown on a shield in their natural colours are blazoned 'proper'.

The colour red in heraldic terms is 'Gules', pronounced with a hard 'G' as in glue rather than a soft 'G' as in gem since the word could then be confused with jewels. Blue can be either Azure which is usually shown as a Cerulean hue, or Bleu celeste which is sky blue and used in the flags of Fiji and Argentina. Green is described simply as Vert. Black is called Sable after the Arctic quadruped whose dark fur is used in the making of artists' paintbrushes. Purple is known as Purpure. There are several other tinctures such as Murrey and Sanguine, which are dark red and earth colours, but these are seldom used because heraldic art is meant to be bright and cheerful.

Gold is referred to as Or, a French word, and is usually painted as yellow although gold-leaf is used on special artwork. The name for silver, Argent, is also taken from the French. This is generally shown as white in paintings as silver-leaf oxidizes quickly and turns black. If metallic silver is required, then platinum, aluminium or white gold is used.

Furs frequently feature in heraldry. Those used most often are: Ermine, which is a white background scattered with black spots; Ermines, which is a black

Fig. 5
A coat of arms

CREST

MANTLING

WREATH

HELM

CORONET

DEXTER
SIDE

SINISTER
SIDE

SHIELD

SUPPORTER

SUPPORTER

MOTTO SCROLL

COMPARTMENT

background with white spots, being the reverse of Ermine; Erminois, which is a gold background with black spots; and Pean, which is a black background with gold ermine spots. Then there are the furs which represent small animal skins sewn together. The animal was probably a squirrel with a blue-grey coat, whose skin was used to line cloaks. These furs are described as Vair, which are blue and white unless described otherwise, and Potent. Several variations of these furs are illustrated in *Plate I*.

   The use of fur provides a colourful and varied means of decorating fields, ordinaries and charges. Again, Ermine is the best-known, being associated with royalty and the nobility. It is represented by a white fur with the black tail ends showing and these can be drawn in many different ways. As before, Ermine can be reversed when white spots are shown on a black background (this is known as Ermines). Other variations include Erminois which is shown as black spots on yellow, and its reverse Pean with yellow spots on a black field. There is also a fur called Erminites which is similar to Ermine but with a red hair on each side of the black spot. This is seldom if ever used in heraldry as it would not be visible from a distance.

The next most important fur is Vair, from the Latin *varus*, and it is found in many forms. It is worth mentioning here that the story of Cinderella's slipper was incorrectly translated some time in the distant past and Vair, meaning fur was wrongly changed to *verre*, meaning glass. The varieties of Vair are shown in *Plate I*: 'Vair', 'Counter-vair', 'Vair of four tinctures', 'Vair in pale', 'Vair en point', and 'alternate Vair'.

The Potent or crutch shape is also classified under furs and is to be found in three varieties, namely 'Potent', 'Counter-potent' and 'Potent-counter-potent', which are also to be seen in *Plate I*.

The use of natural fur in heraldry is seldom seen on the shield except in European armory. In England and Scotland, natural fur is only to be found in representations of coronets and robes of estate. The fur hat of the Sword-bearer of the City of London is also to be seen occasionally.

After the colour of the shield has been given, the principal 'ordinary' or partition of the shield is stated – chevron, bend, bar and so on and its colour or metal is made clear. A simple design with a gold chevron on a blue shield would be blazoned 'Azure a chevron Or'.

After the ordinary has been specified, any charges on the shield or the ordinary must now be clearly explained giving their position, their attitude and their colour. If, for example, the blue shield mentioned above had, in addition to the gold chevron, three silver lion's faces on the shield and on the chevron there were three blue discs, the blazon would be 'Azure on a chevron Or between three lion's heads Argent as many hurts [blue roundels]'.

The crest on top of the helm is described in a similar way, using the same names for the colours and the same terms for the attitudes of beasts and monsters. The crest is always shown upon a wreath of twisted scarves (*Fig. 6*) except when it is issuing out of a crest-coronet. The wreath, as it is called, was originally used to obscure the join between the crest and the top of the helm upon which it was fixed. Leather laces or thongs passed through holes in the top of the helm to secure the crest and mantling and must have been deemed unsightly. The joint was therefore hidden by strips of fabric usually in the colours of the knight's arms, which were wrapped around the top of the helm, and in drawings and paintings of the arms it became part of the crest. The wreath

Fig. 6 A crest with a wreath

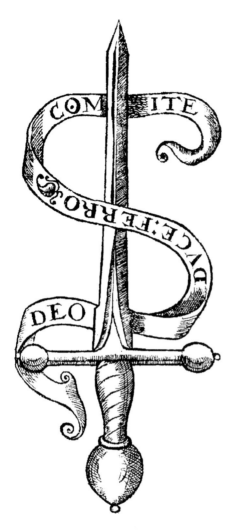

Fig. 7 The badge of Blaise de Montluc, Marshal of France (1592)

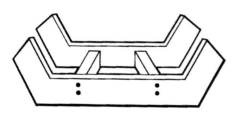

Fig. 8 A drag or sledge, the badge of the Barons Stourton

is always shown with six pieces, the principal metal to the dexter. Sometimes one finds a crest wreath with more than two colours but in every case the metal must come first. In the text of a grant of arms by Letters Patent, the wording states, '. . . and for the Crest upon a wreath [Argent and Gules] . . .'. Without the wreath, the crest could be mistaken for an heraldic badge (*Fig. 7*).

The heraldic badge (*Figs 8 and 9*) is an adjunct to the coat of arms. A badge cannot exist without armorial bearings borne with legal authority. It remains an integral part of an heraldic achievement and cannot exist in isolation. The portcullis was one of the many royal badges of the Tudor dynasty and remains in use today. Ensigned by a royal crown it is used by the House of Lords on a red background as their device and by the House of Commons on a green background. The same badge is used by Somerset Herald, one of Her Majesty's Officers of Arms, while the portcullis without a crown is borne by Portcullis Pursuivant as his official badge. The portcullis is to be seen in many coats of arms, particularly in those of Members of Parliament, and in the coat of the City of Westminster. It is the symbol of defence.

Badges were formerly used by noblemen and great land-owning families both to identify their servants on their different estates and to give their staff a sense of corporate identity. The retainers on one estate would use one particular badge and the retainers on another estate would use another, but all under the umbrella of their master's heraldic prerogative.

There are no restrictions regarding the number of heraldic badges used by a person bearing arms, but it is usually the case for an armiger to have only one or two badges, unless they happen to have inherited more. The majority of modern petitioners for arms do not proceed to the application for a badge, which is regrettable as it precludes them from the use of a full heraldic standard. On a standard, the arms are displayed in the hoist nearest the flag-staff, and the crest and the badge are shown in the long tapered fly, separated usually by two diagonal stripes upon which is written the motto. Any person entitled to arms may place their arms on a square flag in such a way that the design fills the whole area of the flag and this forms their personal banner. The crest does not feature and is only used on a standard. Badges of the armed services appear on flags and these are known as Colours or Standards. The sovereign's flag, generally known as the royal standard, is in fact a banner.

Flags are still a very popular vehicle for heraldry, enlivening and colourfully decorating our streets, civic buildings, offices and even private houses. The contents of the shield should entirely cover the area of an armorial flag which is known as a 'banner'. Helm, crest and mantling should never be shown, and as A.C. Fox-Davies wrote in his *Complete Guide to Heraldry*, in 1909, 'The flag to be flown by a private person, as the law now stands, should bear that person's private arms, if he has any, and if he has not he should be content to forego the pleasure arising from the use of bunting'. Nevertheless, the use of a decorative monogram upon a flag or elsewhere is open to all and is not within the jurisdiction of the College of Arms.

Standards and badges reached their zenith in Tudor times (*Fig. 10*) but they are still allowed and indeed encouraged by the Kings of Arms today as a desirable part of a complete grant of armorial bearings.

One of the best-known royal badges is the three-feather device of the Prince of Wales, possibly used first by the Black Prince, who inherited it from his mother, Philippa of Hainault. The three ostrich feathers are enfiling a gold

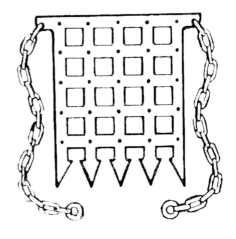

Fig. 9 The portcullis, the symbol of defence

Fig. 10 The Tudor flagship *Mary Rose* wearing flags, gonfalons and pennants with national and personal emblems

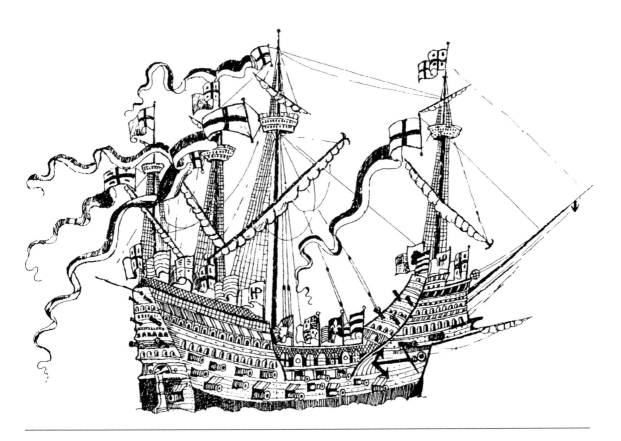

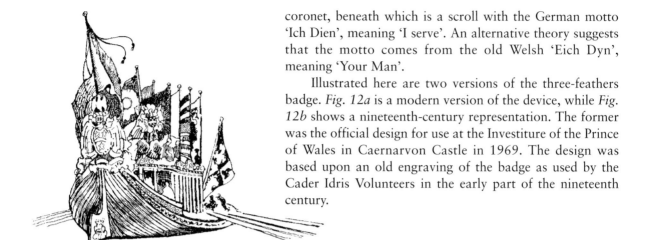

coronet, beneath which is a scroll with the German motto 'Ich Dien', meaning 'I serve'. An alternative theory suggests that the motto comes from the old Welsh 'Eich Dyn', meaning 'Your Man'.

Illustrated here are two versions of the three-feathers badge. *Fig. 12a* is a modern version of the device, while *Fig. 12b* shows a nineteenth-century representation. The former was the official design for use at the Investiture of the Prince of Wales in Caernarvon Castle in 1969. The design was based upon an old engraving of the badge as used by the Cader Idris Volunteers in the early part of the nineteenth century.

Fig. 11 A livery company barge being used by the Lord Mayor of London in a procession on the River Thames in the early nineteenth century

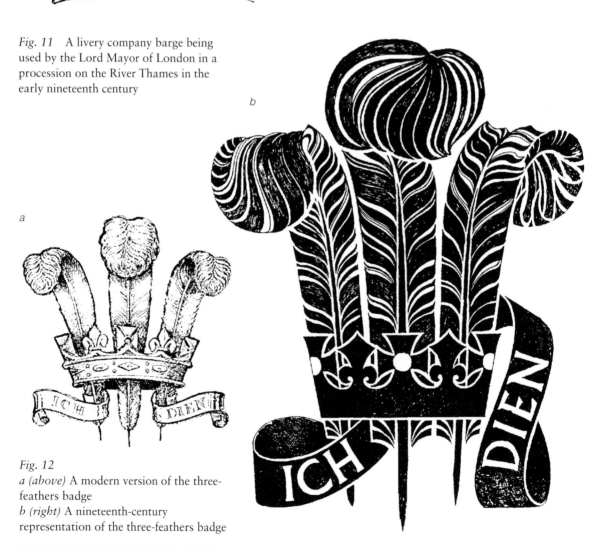

Fig. 12
a (above) A modern version of the three-feathers badge
b (right) A nineteenth-century representation of the three-feathers badge

SHIELDS

THE shield has always been the fighting man's principal means of defence. Without it, a foot-soldier's whole body is vulnerable to attack by an enemy but, with it, he has a tailor-made portable wall to deflect the blows of an assailant and protect himself from danger.

The size and shape of a shield present interesting design problems which have been solved in a number of different ways over the centuries according to the requirements of the time (*Fig. 13*). Using the traditional materials of wood, metal and leather, how did our forebears protect themselves against arrows, sling-shots, spears and swords with an item that is light enough to be carried on one arm?

The answer seems to lie in the ingenious use of laminations of wood and leather reinforced with metal. This combination gave a result that was light, strong and inexpensive. Early shields were made with a timber frame and successive layers of boiled hide were stretched across it and secured at the edges by iron studs. When the leather dried, the surface would have become smooth and hard, making an ideal surface to deflect blows and an equally ideal surface to decorate. Shields made like this would have been lighter and stronger than any others made from the limited range of materials then available.

Having established the method of making and covering a shield that would withstand hard treatment, the next question was its size and its shape. Different kinds of soldiers need different kinds of defence. A foot-soldier needs mobility and his armour was minimal to give him maximum manoeuvrability. An archer needs to stand still to shoot his arrows and while he is standing still, he is at his most vulnerable. Therefore he needs a shield that will protect virtually his whole body and remain standing while he uses both his arms. The mounted soldier needs something different in the form of a smaller shield to protect his left side, giving him enough freedom to control his horse and use his sword. The mounted soldier of knightly rank would have worn armour of some kind, and it is interesting to see that as plate armour developed to cover the whole body, the size of the shield diminished accordingly. By the sixteenth century the shield was little more than a plate with which to parry blows.

a

c

b

NE · CEDE · MALIS

To trace the development of the shield in detail, it is useful to look at examples worldwide and from the earliest times. The greatest problem of course is the lack of documentary evidence relating to an item that would almost inevitably be destroyed within its owner's lifetime. Consequently the only surviving examples of ancient shields were made for ceremonial purposes or for pageants and actual war shields or jousting shields are exceedingly rare. We are therefore almost totally reliant upon graphic representations of ancient shields but at least there is an abundance of such material still available.

The Greek warrior of classical mythology was armed with a short sword and a throwing spear. He wore a helmet, possibly a breastplace or cuirass, a skirt and sandals. He carried a large circular shield which gave him mobility as there are no corners to get in the way, and it was always the right way up. Many illustrations exist on Attic vases and in sculpture which clearly show the form and size of these great shields.

Whereas the Greek warrior was an athlete and needed mobility, the Roman soldier was not an athlete but a solid marching man. His needs were different. The Roman soldier required a curved rectangular shield that fitted his body. When the legion advanced upon the enemy, with the straight sides of the shields interlocked, they presented an impregnable wall against which spears and sling-shots had little effect.

Some of the earliest shields that are easily seen are in the Bayeux tapestry. Although they are not truly of an heraldic nature, they have devices worked upon them. These shields and the tapestry itself were produced before heraldry blossomed in Europe and give us an accurate picture of the designs selected by the soldiers involved. The Norman shields are long and pointed, reaching from a man's face down to well below his knees, and designed primarily as cavalry shields. The upper edge is rounded into a complete semi-circle which runs into straight sides converging in a point at the base of the shield. The surfaces of these kite-shaped shields are decorated with patterns but few symbols or charges. A number of shields show a cross radiating from a central boss, with wavy arms. Others merely have dots or rivets but in two examples there are creatures which resemble wyverns with knotted tails. It is interesting that the long Norman shields imported into England at the time of the conquest immediately superseded the smaller circular infantry shields used by the Anglo-Saxons at the time.

Fig. 13 Shield shapes:
a Eighteenth-century cartouche
b Nineteenth-century decorative shield
c European-style shield

CRESTS

THE heraldic crest, derived from the Latin *crista*, meaning a cockscomb, is the three-dimensional device that was secured to the top of the helm. It was attached by means of straps and laces which were hidden by the crest-wreath and mantling. The wreath was formed from two lengths of coloured cloth or scarves twisted together which concealed the join between crest and helm. From the wreath flowed the mantling, a decorative cloak attached to the rear of the helm to protect the wearer from inclement elements.

What was the purpose of the crest? The first, I think, was vanity. At the time when the fan crest was first used, it had no decoration so therefore it was not intended for identification and was merely a showpiece. It would have added to the height of the rider and made him more awesome in appearance. Secondly, when crests did assume a three-dimensional form and reflected the arms of its owner, they would have, of course, been a great help in identifying mounted men, especially at crowded tournaments where the shield and horse-trappings were obscured by spectators standing in the way. Indeed at some tournaments crests were obligatory and were inspected and recorded before the event.

The crest originated as a flat fan-like object laced to the top of the helm for no particular heraldic reason other than personal decoration, and examples may be seen on early seals such as the one shown in *Fig. 14*. The Earl of Arundel used a flat semi-circular fan crest in the early part of the fourteenth century, as did the Prince of Wales and the Earl of Hereford. One must assume that the crests were made from leather but none are still in existence for us to examine. They

Fig. 14   From the seal of Richard Fitzalan, Earl of Arundel (1301)

are, however, to be seen in illustrated manuscripts from which it appears that at a later stage the fans were gilded and painted. It was a natural progression for the painted decoration to reflect the arms borne on the shield of the wearer and on his horse-trappings.

It is possible that the next stage in the development of the crest was the cutting out of a shape, be it an animal or an object, so that a flat decoration which we would recognize as an heraldic crest was secured to the helm rather than a fan. Contemporary illustrations do not make it entirely clear how much modelling existed at this stage, and the artists of the time might well have used their imaginations in portraying fully three-dimensional figures. Nevertheless it seems clear that fully-modelled crests were in general use by the middle of the fourteenth century. Crests were being used throughout Europe at this time, with particular enthusiasm and flair being demonstrated in Germany. There the crests developed along slightly different lines favouring wings and feathers which resembled the earlier fan crests, and buffalo horns which were later represented as elephant trunks (see *Plate IXd*).

Early crests were simple and imaginative, being essentially practical items of a knight's equipment. They were modelled from light timber, wire and boiled leather which, when dry, formed a lightweight but strong skin similar to modern shoe-leather. This could be painted and gilded and would be inexpensive, the principal expense being the skill of the craftsman. The crest would be long-lasting if it was not damaged, as is shown by the crest of the Black Prince in Canterbury Cathedral which has survived for over 600 years.

As practical items of heraldry, crests ceased to be made with the demise of the tournament except for funeral pageants. They had, however, become hereditary and were continued in use in decorative heraldry as an integral part of a coat of arms. Without the need to meet the special requirements of mounted knights in full armour, crests became more complicated in design and in some cases would have been impossible to construct. Small insignificant items were often placed around, or in front of, the main feature of the crest and were even hung in space over the crest. A good example of a bad crest is that of Drake which has a terrestrial globe with a ship upon it in full sail being pulled by a ribbon which is held by a hand issuing from the clouds (*Fig. 15*). It is easy to understand the symbolism, but impossible to make as a device for a helm.

Fig. 15　Sir Francis Drake's crest

Fig. 16   Examples of traditional crests

Efforts are being made in all aspects of contemporary armoury to return to simple designs wherever possible and although we cannot return to the dawn of heraldry, much improvement has been made in the last hundred years.

Various examples of traditional crests are shown in *Fig. 16*.

SUPPORTERS

HERALDIC supporters are the beasts, humans or other items that appear on either side of a shield to support it. Not everyone entitled to arms is entitled to supporters. These are primarily reserved for peers of the realm, knights of the highest rank and corporate bodies of national standing. There are of course some exceptions. The granting of supporters gives greater honour and status to the coat of arms and to its bearer.

To discover the origin of supporters, one must look at early seals where the armorial shield placed in a circle creates a space on either side. This is filled either with foliage or with animals of some kind, and encourages the theory that supporters, which were later granted as part of the coat of arms, originated in this way. Although supporters were used in conjunction with the armorial bearings of Edward III and Richard II, they are not generally found before the reign of Henry VIII, even for peers of the realm.

Beasts and human figures (*Fig. 17*) are the principal source of inspiration for supporters which are two in number in England and Scotland, although single supporters are sometimes used in Europe. The City of Southampton, however, employs the sterns of two sailing-ships with lions standing on them for its supporters (*Fig. 18*). The best-known supporters are the lion and the unicorn which support the royal arms of the United Kingdom (see *Plate X*).

The livery companies of the City of London use supporters, among which is an interesting example of an unusual creature. The armorial bearings (*Fig. 20*) of the Worshipful Company of Fishmongers has 'a Mereman his upper parts armed his nether part of a fyshe, all naturall, in

Fig. 17 Wild man or savage, as a supporter

his right hande holdinge a faucheon and with his left susteyninge the Heaulme and Tymbre: And on the left syde of the sayde Armes a Mermayde with her right hand supporting the Armes and in her lefte bearinge a mirrour or looking glasse all in proper colour'.

The Worshipful Company of Skinners has a grant of supporters made in 1550 by Thomas Hawley, Clarenceux King of Arms, which shows the shield held by a lizard and a martin, each with a wreath of laurel around their necks. The City of London has dragons. The Worshipful Company of Painter-Stainers has two panthers incensed, the coloured roundels on their bodies representing daubs of paints on the smocks of the apprentice painters (*Fig. 19* and *Plate II*).

Fig. 18   The supporters of the City of Southampton's arms are sailing ships

Fig. 19   The armorial bearings of the Worshipful Company of Painter-Stainers

Fig. 20   The armorial bearings of the Worshipful Company of Fishmongers

THEORY OF HERALDIC ART

THERE have always been various requirements that the heraldic artist must understand and adhere to if he or she is going to produce successful work. Symbolism, exaggeration and stylization all play their part in the heraldic art, but the principal rule is to fill the space on the shield boldly so that the charges fit comfortably within its confines. Shield shapes vary (see *Fig. 13*, page 24), so it is essential that the artist has a grasp of proportion and dimension and yet appreciates the flexibility that the disciplines of heraldic art offer.

It is good advice to study the work of early heraldic artists who seemed to have a natural understanding of balance and colour. The ancient rolls of arms in the College of Arms and the British Museum show that the first or second generation of artists knew how to dispose their charges liberally across the shield without wasting space or overcrowding. The colouring, though subdued after hundreds of years, still shows a sensitive approach to the spectrum of raw tinctures available from vegetable and mineral pigments.

This book is not intended to be a workshop manual, for practical experience cannot be gained from books, any more than the technique of fly-fishing can be learned in a library. Nevertheless I hope that it may draw attention to certain aspects of heraldic art which may not have previously been apparent to you. For example, the width of a fess or a bend depends upon the shape and dimensions of the shield, and no formulae will provide the exact answer. The final decision is up to the artist who must base their artwork on experience and a practised eye. How dark can you make the colour red before it becomes Murrey or even Sanguine? We all see colours slightly differently, and no rules will provide the answer.

Successful heraldic design lies in the judgement of proportion, balance, colour and disciplined boldness. These virtues were innate in the early heraldic artists and it is encouraging to see that artistic standards are steadily rising from the low standards of the eighteenth and nineteenth centuries. Form and texture play an important part in the representation of a coat of arms, particularly in present times when so many new materials are available to the artist and craftsman. We must not however merely criticize but try to be creative and constructive.

HATCHING

ONE method of indicating colours and metals on a shield is by the use of very fine lines drawn or engraved in different directions to identify the tinctures. This system is called hatching, from the French word *hacher*, meaning to cut or hack into small pieces, and is not to be confused with hatchment, which is a funeral painting and is a corruption of the word achievement. With familiarity of the different forms of hatching (*Figs. 21–25*) and a little experience, every piece of heraldically engraved silver and every properly hatched black and white bookplate can with imagination be visualized in colour.

Funereal hatchments are lozenge-shaped paintings of the coats of arms of deceased persons. They are usually painted on stretched canvas like an ordinary oil painting, or on timber panels, and measure between two and five feet square. After the death of an armiger a hatchment was painted and hung over the front door of his house to inform visitors and passing travellers of the sad event. The hatchment would be removed from the house a few months later and displayed in the local church as a memorial. Many hatchments are still to be found in churches today, long after this quaint heraldic custom died out. This was the last vestige of the full heraldic funeral which is outside the scope of this book. The background to the coat of arms on a hatchment is painted black but if the arms are impaled with those of a spouse who is still living, then his or her background is painted white. Symbols of mortality such as skulls and bones were often included in the paintings, together with mottoes and legends such as *Resurgam*.

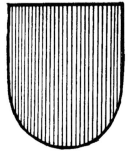

Fig. 21   Vertical lines for red (Gules)

Another system used for identifying colours is merely to abbreviate the heraldic name for the colour, and this is known as 'tricking'. The term comes from the French word *trique*, meaning an ingenious or peculiar way of doing something. In this method, Gules becomes 'gu', Vert 'vt', Sable 'sa', Azure 'az', proper 'ppr', and so on, except where confusion might occur. Azure is also often shortened to 'b' for blue, as the abbreviation 'az' could be mistaken for 'arg' which is silver. When drafting a blazon, it is sometimes better to say gold than 'or', as this could be confused with the disjunctive particle.

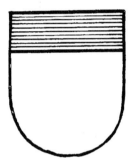

Fig. 22
a horizontal lines for blue (Azure)
b plain for silver (Argent)

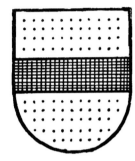

Fig. 23
a dots for gold or yellow (Or)
b cross-hatching vertically and horizontally for black (Sable)

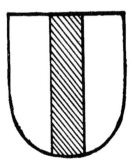

Fig. 24 Lines diagonally from dexter chief to sinister base for green (Vert)

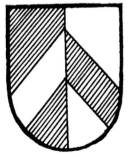

Fig. 25 Lines from sinister chief to dexter base for purple (Purpure)

PARTITION LINES

A N HERALDIC shield is divided into several parts by partition lines which are also used to define the outline of the various ordinaries used in heraldry. *Fig. 26* shows the exact nature of each line described below.

a ENGRAILED From the French word *grêler*, meaning to hail. A line indented with curves or semi-circles forming valleys and cusps as if bruised by hailstones.

b NEBULY A line that is cloud-like, with edges resembling the nodules on a jigsaw puzzle piece.

c INVECTED The opposite to engrailed. A line formed from convex arcs or scallops.

d DOVETAILED A line comprised of tapered pieces resembling the dovetailed joint of a cabinet-maker.

e EMBATTLED A line that looks like the battlements of a castle wall, having crenellations and embrasures.

f FLORY-COUNTER-FLORY A line decorated with fleurs-de-lys pointing inwards and outwards alternately.

g RAYONNÉ A line that is formed from wavy pointed flames.

h POTENTÉ A line made from 'T' shapes, and their reverse, derived from the old word 'potent' meaning a crutch.

i DANCETTY A line made from zigzag 'V' shapes pointing alternately up and down.

j RAGULY A rustic line representing the trunk of a tree with the branches cut off, hence 'ragged'. The heraldic badge of the Earls of Warwick is a bear holding a ragged staff.

k WAVY An undulating line often used to represent water.

l INDENTED A line having sawtooth indentations smaller than the dog-tooth points of dancetty.

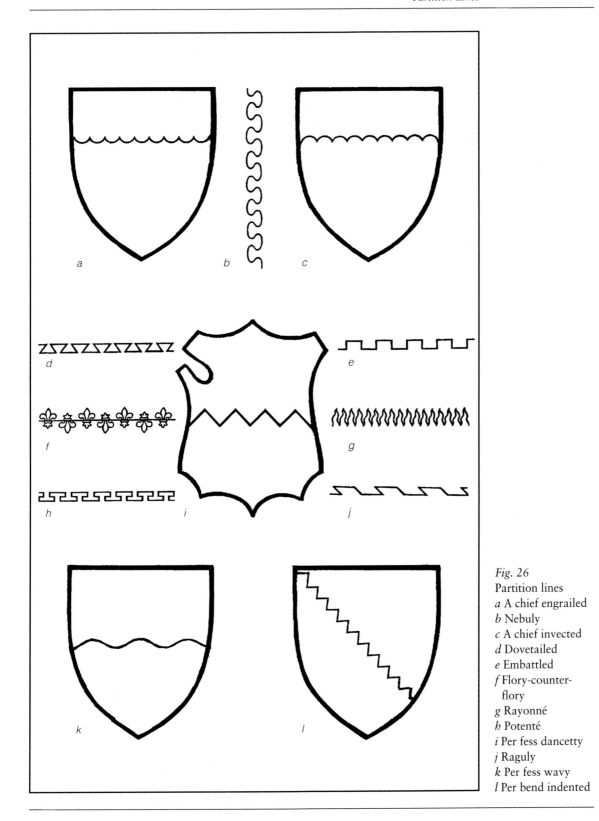

Fig. 26
Partition lines
a A chief engrailed
b Nebuly
c A chief invected
d Dovetailed
e Embattled
f Flory-counter-
    flory
g Rayonné
h Potenté
i Per fess dancetty
j Raguly
k Per fess wavy
l Per bend indented

ORDINARIES AND SUB-ORDINARIES

THE heraldic division of a shield of the simplest, earliest and commonest kind is probably derived from the basic construction of a shield made from timber and hide. Several of these divisions have over the centuries been placed in categories called ordinaries (honourable or greater) and sub-ordinaries (diminutives). Their importance for the heraldic artist lies not in their historic or academic provenance, but in their widths and their angles. The following brief notes about each ordinary describe how a shield is properly divided. Where a shield is dissected vertically, horizontally or diagonally, it is referred to as 'per' pale or 'per' bend, etc. If a charge is placed on a bend, it is drawn at the same angle as the bend and not vertically.

BEND *(Fig. 27)* A stripe running diagonally across the shield from dexter chief to sinister base, originally from bind, or bond. Generally shown in breadth to contain a fifth part of the surface of the shield but, if charged, a third part of the shield.

BAR *(Fig. 28)* 'A piece of wood, metal or other rigid material, long in proportion to its thickness, and frequently used as a barrier, fastening or obstruction. Like the Fess, but narrower and including the fifth part or less of the field.' *O.E.D.* A horizontal or transverse stripe across the shield. Popular legend refers to a bar sinister being the sign of illegitimacy, but as a bar is horizontal, it cannot be either dexter or sinister. The usual sign of illegitimacy (in England) is a bordure wavy or compony, or a baton sinister.

FESS or FESSE *(Fig. 29)* A horizontal band running across the centre of a shield taking up about one-third of the area. From the Latin word *fascia* meaning a band, now used to describe the horizontal board above shop windows displaying the name of the shop.

CHIEF *(Fig. 30)* The head, top or upper end of the shield taking up one-third of the field shield (fifteenth century). A horizontal line dividing the upper part of the

Fig. 27   Bend

Fig. 28   Bar

Fig. 29   Fess

Fig. 30   Chief

shield from the main part, an area considered to be held in honour, reflecting its appellation of head, chief, principal, etc. The only other place on a shield of similar or even greater account is 'Honour Point' in the centre of the field.

PALE *(Fig. 31)* A vertical stripe running down the centre of the shield occupying about one-third of the area. The word palisade, meaning vertical stakes or planks, has the same origin.

LOZENGE *(Fig. 33a, b, c* and *d)* Derived from the old French word *lauza*, a tombstone, the lozenge *(Fig. 32a)* is a diamond-shaped device slightly taller than its width. When a lozenge is pierced with its own shape, it is a mascle *(Fig. 32b)*, and when it is pierced with a circular hole, it is a rustre *(Fig. 32c)*. A narrower version is called a fusil *(Fig. 32d)*. The lozenge shape is used for the display of the arms of spinsters and widows, who, as females, had no use for a shield. The lozenge is also used in the display of funeral hatchments.

LABEL *(Fig. 32)* The label of three points may be used as a charge, or as the cadency mark of an eldest son. If it is borne as a cadency mark, it may be any colour except white which is reserved for the eldest son of the sovereign.

CHEVRON *(Fig. 34)* An angled or pitched device taking up about one-third of the shield, issuing from the sides and forming a point in the centre, in the manner of an inverted 'V'. Possibly from the old French *chèvre*, a musk deer, whose slot would form the shape of a chevron in the earth. French chevrons sometimes are inverted, whereas English chevrons are never shown in this position.

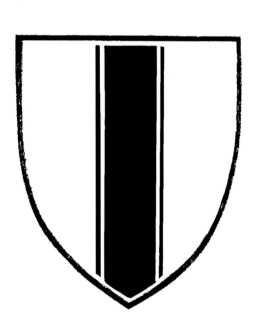

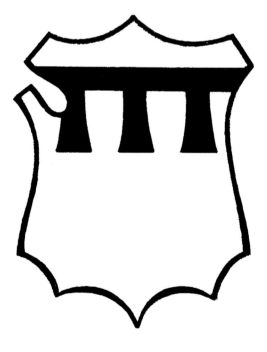

Fig. 31   Pale   *Fig. 32*   Label

Fig. 33a   Lozenge

Fig. 33b   Mascle

Fig. 33c   Rustre

Fig. 33d   Fusil

Fig. 34 Chevron

Fig. 35 Saltire

Fig. 36 Cross

Fig. 37 Pile

SALTIRE *(Fig. 35)* This is the cross of St Andrew, which dissects the field from the four 'corners' of the shield.

CROSS *(Fig. 36)* This, of course, is the symbol of the Christian faith and was borne on the surcoats and shields of the crusaders. No symbol is more easily recognized and understood than the red cross on a white field, for the church, St George and England. Very many versions of the cross are to be seen in heraldry (see *Fig. 52*, page 46).

PILE *(Fig. 37)* A triangular shape issuing from the top of the shield, and its point in the base, the upper horizontal taking up nearly the whole width of the shield. The pile may also issue from the flanks of the shield but if it rises from the base, it is termed a 'pile reversed'. The sides of the pile are subject to the usual lines of partition and it may be borne singly or in numbers which must be correctly stated.

SHAKEFORK or PALL *(Fig. 38)* A 'Y'-shaped device originating from the vestment known as a pallium and worn by priests. It comprises a narrow band of white wool worn about the shoulders. It has two short pendants, one hanging down the front and the other at the back decorated with six black crosses. It is a symbol of papal authority and may be given by the Pope to archbishops to indicate their participation in his authority. Hence it is a device signifying rank within the church, and may be seen in the arms of the Archiepiscopal Sees of Canterbury, Armagh and Dublin.

FRET *(Fig. 39)* A popular device formed from battens in lozenge pierced by two strips interlaced in saltire. The fret resembles the knot made by Morris dancers with their battens. When the pattern is repeated over the entire surface of the shield, it is termed 'fretty' and looks like a net.

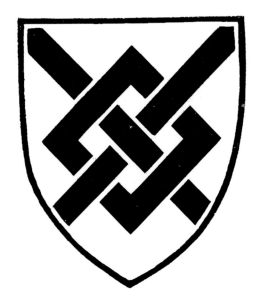

Fig. 38 Shakefork or pall

Fig. 39 Fret

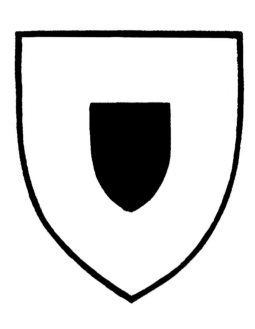

Fig. 40   Escutcheon

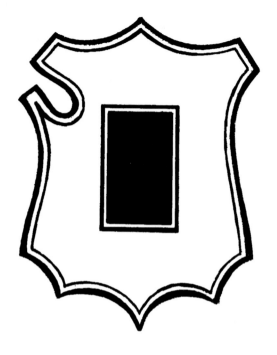

Fig. 41   Billet

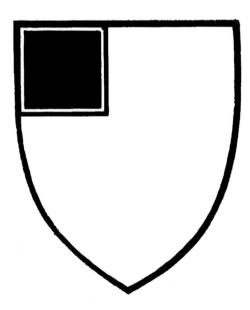

Fig. 42   Canton

Fig. 43   Quarter

ESCUTCHEON *(Fig. 40)* A miniature shield placed upon the field in a different colour or metal. Its shape should conform to the contours of the parent shield.

BILLET *(Fig. 41)* A small rectangular shape resembling a block of wood or metal.

CANTON *(Fig. 42)* The diminutive of the quarter and borne in the chief of a shield. It often reflects a reward for valour or merit and can be granted as an augmentation of honour. The canton is always shown superimposed over all other ordinaries and charges.

QUARTER *(Fig. 43)* The fourth part of a shield divided per cross and usually blazoned 'per cross' with the particular tincture given. For example, the De Vere family, Earls of Oxford, bear 'Quarterly Gules and Or in the first Quarter a mullet Argent'.

GYRON *(Fig. 44)* A triangular device in the first quarter of a shield divided per bend, reaching into the centre of the shield and having a horizontal base. Gyronny is a sub-division of the shield per cross and per saltire forming eight triangular wedges.

FLANCHE (Flasques, or Voiders) *(Fig. 45)* A device always borne in pairs, being curved lines or radii issuing from the flanks of a shield, forming a space between them resembling the core of an apple.

CHAPLET *(Fig. 46a, b and c)* A very pretty device which is really a garland or wreath, composed of leaves and flowers. Four roses are usually shown in the arrangement, one at the top and the bottom and one on either side. This is not to be confused with the olive crown *(a)* or civic crown *(b)* which is made up from oak-leaves and acorns. The triumphal crown *(c)* is made from laurel and takes the same form.

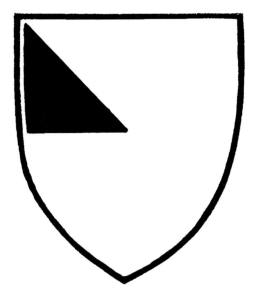

Fig. 44 Gyron   *Fig. 45* Flanche

Fig. 47   Annulet

Fig. 46a   Olive crown

Fig. 48   Bordure

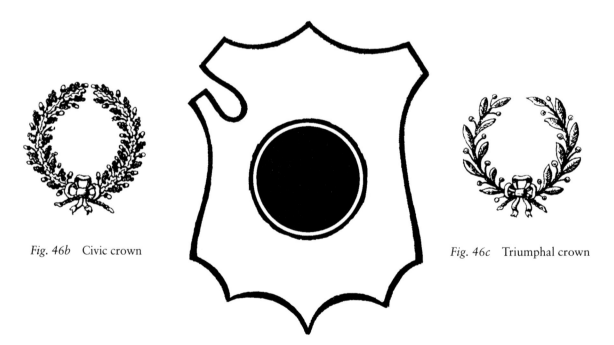

Fig. 46b   Civic crown

Fig. 46c   Triumphal crown

Fig. 49   Roundel

ROUNDEL *(Fig. 49)* A circular disc of any colour or metal, all of which have their own name. When a roundel is gold, representing a coin, it is termed a 'bezant'. When it is white or silver, it is a 'plate'. When red (Gules) it is a 'torteau'. When blue (Azure) it is a 'hurt'. When a roundel is black (Sable) it is termed an 'ogress' or a gun-stone or pellet, which is presumably a cannon-ball. When a roundel is purple, it is called a 'golpe' and when it is green (Vert), it is a 'pomeis'. If the roundel is Tenné, it is called an 'orange' and in the rare case of it being shown Sanguine, it is called a 'guze'. If the roundel is white with wavy blue bars upon it, it is termed a 'fountain' and is to be seen in many coats of arms that reflect proximity to springs, wells, etc.

ANNULET *(Fig. 47)* A ring of any colour borne singly or in multiples either isolated or interlinked with each other. Annulets could be blazoned as pierced Roundels, and must not be confused with 'gem-rings' which must show a gemstone.

BORDURE *(Fig. 48)* Literally a border running round the perimeter of the shield and used in Scotland as a mark of cadency.

ORLE *(Fig. 50)* A narrow border set within the shield following the edge, but unlike the bordure it does not reach the edge. When small charges are placed around the edge of the shield they are said to be 'in orle'.

TRESSURE *(Fig. 51)* A double diminutive of the orle which may be described as tramlines following the perimeter of the shield. The lines are less broad than an orle and the tincture or metal of the shield shows between them. The best-known example is seen in the royal arms of Scotland where the red lion of the country is displayed within a double tressure decorated with fleur-de-lys blazoned as a 'double tressure flory-counter-flory'.

Fig. 50   Orle

Fig. 51   Double tressure flory-counter-flory

a   b   c   d   e

f   g   h   i   j

k   l   m   n   o

p   q   r   s   t

u   v   w   x   y

CROSSES

a PLAIN CROSS THROUGHOUT The Cross of St George.

b LONG CROSS or PASSION CROSS.

c CALVARY CROSS With three steps or 'grieces', sometimes referred to as 'degrees'.

d PATRIARCHAL CROSS The upper limb is crossed with a small cross-bar.

e CROSS HUMETTY The arms of the cross are couped or cut-off and do not reach the edge of the shield.

f MALTESE CROSS With four arms terminating in eight points.

g CROSS MOLINE A cross, the arms of which terminate in two expanded and curved branches which resemble the extremities of a mill-rind.

h CROSS PATÉE QUADRATE.

i CROSS PATONCE.

j CROSS PATÉE (also called Formée) This cross together with fleurs-de-lys appears on the rim of English royal crowns.

k CROSS QUARTER-PIERCED.

l CROSS POMMÉ or POMELLED Made up from four sword hilts with pommels.

m CROSS POTENT The ancient name for a crutch was a 'potent'.

n CROSS BOTANY The ends of the arms terminating in simple leaves.

o CROSS CROSSLET.

p TAU CROSS (St Anthony's Cross) From the Greek letter 'T'.

q CROSS FLORY The ends of the arms terminate in fleurs-de-lys.

r CROSS PATÉE FITCHY The lower arm is sharpened to a point.

s CROSS HUMETTY FLORY.

t CROSS POTENT CROSSED.

u CROSS CERCELÉ or RECERCELÉ.

v CROSS PATÉE FLORETTY.

w CROSS TRIPARTED AND FRETTED.

x CROSS AVELANE A cross formed from four hazelnuts in their frilly husks (1611).

y A FYLFOT.

Fig. 52 Crosses

CHARGES AND FIELD SPORTS

CONSIDERING that the majority of country squires and gentry were constantly engaged in field sports, it is surprising that such pursuits are represented by comparatively few designs in heraldry. Fishing was an essential part of medieval life but its purpose was survival and not recreation. Hunting, as we know it today, did not exist except for the boar and the deer, with distant memories and tales of the wolf. The oldest form of hunting on foot still exists and the hare is still pursued today by packs of beagles and basset-hounds, although otter-hunting has now been banned. The features of the heraldic Talbot remain in our bloodhounds which are still recognizable as Barlow's Southern-mouthed Hounds.

Heraldry reflects the sport of the old gentry with boar-spears, bugle-horns and stags' heads, together with the paraphernalia of falconry. Of all field sports, falconry remains supreme in providing a wealth of words and expressions not only to heraldry but to the English language in general. Heraldry and falconry have always been closely allied and at one time were considered to be essential parts of the education of a young gentleman. The *Boke of St Albans*, reputedly written by Dame Juliana de Berners, whose authorship is now refuted, was subtitled *Hunting, Hawking and Heraldry*. The current theory is that it was written by the Schoolmaster Printer of St Albans in 1486. Nevertheless, birds of prey with their trappings and equipment often appear. The following brief glossary of terms used in falconry may therefore be useful to an armorist wishing to appreciate the finer points of detail. This list is by no means complete but should suffice for the heraldic enthusiast.

BEWIT The small leather strap that attaches the bells to the legs of the hawk.

FLIGHTS or PENNES The primary or flight-feathers used by any bird for flying and from which pens were made.

HAWK-BELLS These are always spherical and usually made of brass. They help the falconer to locate a lost bird. The bells are attached to the leg of the hawk with leather straps.

HOOD A leather cap which is placed upon a hawk's head to blindfold it (hood-winked).

JESSES Flat leather straps attached to both legs of a hawk. 'Though that her jesses were my dear heart-strings.' (*Othello*, Act III, scene iii.)

LEASH A leather thong which is passed through the swivel to serve as a lead.

LURE A decoy made from two wings which, when flown from a line, entices the falcon to return to its owner.

POUNCES The talons of a falcon.

SWIVEL A metal connector at the end of the jesses that allows the leash and the jesses to remain untwisted.

VARVELS Flat metal discs that were used before swivels were invented. They were made of brass or silver and sometimes had the owner's initials or crest engraved upon them.

HELMS

THREE basic kinds of helms are used in heraldry. Although it is very tempting to consider the history of the helm and to trace its development through the centuries, it is not essential to do so in this book. Most people interested in armory know that the steel tilting-helm of the fifteenth-century is used in profile by gentlemen and esquires, that knights and baronets display a visored helm affronté with the visor raised and that peers of the realm and royalty use a barred pageant helm in silver and gold. What is of concern to the artist and the designer is the axis of the helm and crest, the shape of the helm, its proportion and the overall position regarding the crest and the shield. In Scotland the 'pot-helm', illustrated in *Plate IXa*, is much used and reflects a style of armour in vogue for both jousting and warfare from the Crusades until the end of the thirteenth century.

The gentlemen's tilting helm, illustrated in *Plate IXc*, is in appearance the simplest of all helms and its stark sculptured lines make it both handsome and menacing. The angle of the sight or vision slit and the jutting lip of the reinforced buff gives the helm a forbidding featureless appearance. Indeed these helms are sometimes referred to as 'frog-mouthed' helms but the usual term is Great Helm. They were formed from three pieces of metal riveted together. The domed skull forming the cap was forged in one piece with a curved plate fixed to it and descending to cover the back of the head and the neck. The face-guard was then fitted to this by means of flanges and round-headed rivets. In heraldry two rivets are generally shown on the flanges with several rivets down the side of the helm which are usually gilded. For the sake of realism, several holes are shown for lacing the lining which protected the wearer's head. A charnel or buckle was fixed to the front to secure the helm to the breastplate. A small part of the quilted lining to the helm usually shows beneath the shoulder-plate and within the visor. This is generally tinted red although any colour can be used.

Most existing examples of Great Helms have been constructed in three parts but one helm exists that is amazingly wrought from only two plates of metal. Several Great Helms exist including the Brocas helm, illustrated in *Plate IXb*, in the Tower Armouries, and also in the Wallace Collection, at Coleshill, in Melbury Sampford church in Dorset and at Wingfield Digby.

An important consideration for any artist is the axis of the crest on top of the helm. The simple rule is that the helm should be shown in profile but in reality it is often turned slightly towards the viewer. If the crest is drawn in profile, this is fine but the crest is essentially a three-dimensional object and cannot always be shown in profile with ease. Therefore the crest should be shown in a convenient way and the helm beneath it turned until the two items are on the same axis. A further difficulty arises if the helm has to be turned 45 degrees and is in consequence affronté, a position that does not officially exist in heraldry for close-helms. Current practice, however, shows that the present Kings of Arms who have the final word in the matter, at least in the representation on the Letters Patent, are increasingly inclined to look favourably on a logical solution to the problem, rather than keeping to the letter of the heraldic law.

The Great Helm was designed to deflect and protect. All armour except for the earliest was designed to turn aside an opponent's weapon and the great tilting helm is a marvellous example of the smith's art and skill in producing a piece of protective headgear that has no angles or crevices where a sword or lance-point might lodge. The pointed face-plate cut through the air like the bows of an ocean liner during the charge when the rider's head was lowered. Just before impact the head was raised obscuring the rider's vision but presenting his opponent with a flawless casing of streamlined steel. This beautiful design was developed in the second decade of the sixteenth century when a 'chin' was added to the face-plate and hatches and trap-doors were built into the helms for ventilation and communication. These innovations no doubt made life more comfortable for the person inside the armour, but the majestic clean lines of the earlier Great Helms were lost. These helms were made from iron or steel and would have been scoured with finely ground sand and oil, so the surface did not have a mirror finish but was highly burnished to a bright metallic sheen replete with the scars of combat.

CORONETS OF RANK

THE United Kingdom is the only country in the world where coronets are actually worn and then only at the coronation of a new sovereign. Each rank of the peerage has its own type of coronet which is shown in a coat of arms above the helm. The only other people able to have coronets or crowns are the Kings of Arms of England and Scotland. 'Crest coronets' do not signify rank and are borne by many families. These have three strawberry leaves and can be of any colour.

The royal crown as depicted in heraldic art is the crown of St Edward, and is only used at a coronation. The Imperial State Crown is worn by H.M. the Queen once a year at the State Opening of Parliament. The basic form of both crowns is the same, being a rim set with crosses patée and fleur-de-lys and having two arches supporting a small orb or mound. Within the crown is a velvet cap lined with ermine which is turned up beneath the rim. The coronets of peers of the realm, illustrated in *Plate X*, broadly follow this style, having silver gilt rims with strawberry leaves or silver balls called pearls and a velvet cap lined with ermine, but no arches.

MANTLING

MANTLING is the decorative fabric covering to the helm much used by artists in their creative representation of coats of arms, and sometimes irreverently referred to as 'seaweed'. Its purpose is very practical in that it was a cover for the Great Helm and protected both its wearer from the sun and the burnished steel helm from the more destructive elements. In recent times, the kepi headgear of the French Foreign Legion and the topi of the British Army were both made with a fabric veil to cover the nape of the wearer's neck, and both, in a way, evolved from the capeline, a woollen hood for the head or a skull cap worn in medieval times.

Examples of early mantling may be seen on monumental brasses and on the Garter stall-plates in Windsor Castle. The earliest stall-plate was erected for Ralph, Lord Bassett, K.G. (1368–90), illustrated in *Plate XIc*), and shows a very simple form of mantling. The fabric fits closely to the top of the helm and hangs at the back in a straight fall with scalloped edge terminating in a large tassel. No lining is shown and there are none of the convolutions or graceful curves that quickly developed in the following century. Thirty years after the death of Lord Bassett, the style of mantling used on the stall-plates had changed dramatically and on the plate put up for Richard Wydville, Lord Rivers, the swirling mantling is full of movement and action. It is coloured red, scattered with gold trefoils and has large tassels at the ends of the fronds. The crest is a demi-man holding a scimitar aloft in his right hand. His costume is the same fabric as the mantling, the long sleeves descending below the helm and combining with the mantling to give a stiking visual effect.

On these ancient representations of heraldry, where the crest is a bird or some other creature adorned with feathers, the mantling is often feathered in a similar manner to create a compact visual image where the crest is bonded to the mantling through its colour and surface texture.

During the fifteenth century the colours red and white, or Gules doubled Argent, became increasingly popular and remained so until livery colours were substituted in the seventeenth century. In Scotland, Gules and Argent were retained until 1890. Until fairly recently in England the mantling of peers of the realm was Gules lined with Ermine and this still pertains in Scotland, although the wreath is usually shown in the livery colours.

The wreath, which will be seen under all crests without crest coronets, was formed from two scarves twisted together and encircled the helm at the point where the crest was laced on. It was a convenient way of hiding the join between crest and helm and in due course became an integral part of the crest. The wreath is now shown with six pieces visible in the correct livery colours. The first piece to the dexter is always shown in the principal metal of the livery and the second piece in the principal tincture or colour of the livery. This is the means of determining the livery colours of any particular family and until the beginning of the twentieth century, various reference books specified the correct livery colours for families to dress their footmen.

Mantling is undergoing a period of rejuvenation and more invention is being shown in design. It is not unusual now to see three colours in the wreath with differed coloured mantling on either side of the helm. The ancient and cheerful conceit of powdering the mantling with many badges has been revived but I cannot recall having seen feathered mantling in recent years.

During the sixteenth century, mantling was often portrayed as an actual mantle, usually in red with a white fur lining opening up with the shield suspended within it. Elaborate cords and tassels held the upper corners in decorative bunches and sometimes the ermine bars of a peer's parliamentary robe were shown. This style of mantling, which was at the discretion of the artist, persisted until the nineteenth century and was popular with people who wished to display their arms in a flamboyant and rather pompous manner; it looks best in conjunction with the coronet of a peer of the realm.

The use of this style of mantling has always been more acceptable in Europe than in Great Britain. In the case of royal families and the high nobility, where the mantle is an hereditary privilege, supporters and even banners are depicted within the robe. In the very grandest examples the mantle becomes a tent or pavilion with an extra peak or dome beneath the crown. In these elaborate representations the outer sides of the robe are curled back to reveal the arms embroidered on the reverse. In Spain a small mantle or 'mantelele' is sometimes used, usually red lined with ermine, descending from the helm on only one side of the shield.

Fig. 53 The Stourton crest, showing mantling

The mantling of a coat of arms has always given the artist the widest rein to demonstrate his creative skills and yet, as part of an achievement, it is the least important part. It is in the mantling that we can relish the most extravagant seventeenth- and eighteenth-century carving, not least in the glory of the many royal arms to be found in English churches proclaiming faith and loyalty.

I would argue that a special category of mantling exists where it forms part of and an extension of the crest. Many examples exist until the fifteenth century in England and Scotland, and in Europe where it found particular favour. Again the German artists and heralds were prolific and brilliant in their sheer invention. A good English example is the crest of Stourton (*Fig. 53*), which is a Cistercian monk wielding a scourge. His habit descends below the helm to form the mantling. Another example is found in the arms of Man, where the crest is a human leg erect habited in chain-mail. The mail covering the thigh continues downwards through a crest coronet and forms a short mantling. The German 'Kantze' Roll in Constance illustrates many good examples.

Many fine examples of freedom and movement within mantling are to be seen in the work of Albrecht Dürer (1471–1528) and his followers. These black and white engravings have a vitality and energy that have hardly been matched in the graphic representation of shields, crests and mantling. One particular example (*Fig. 54)* shows a mastless, beached cog or ship on the shield and, for the crest issuing from a crest coronet, the mast of a ship with a fighting-top and a pennant flying, the sail billowing to the sinister. The main feature, however, is the treatment of the mantling which, although unmistakably floral, is an amazing representation of foaming surf and crashing breakers.

Another example *(Fig. 56)* of movement in mantling is also by Dürer and depicts a hunting scene by moonlight. The huntsman who is some kind of satyr judging by his hooves, is running with his hounds and blowing his horn. Because of the way the mantling is drawn, he appears to be chasing through a clearing in the forest. The animation and movement of the whole engraving is lent such vitality by the angle of the shield and the mantling that the demi-man crest is convincingly extending his left arm to balance the work and prevent it from rushing off the page to the dexter.

A fine static drawing (*Fig. 57)* of arms and crest by Dürer shows a noblewoman, possibly a widow, regarding a shield and helm with crest and mantling suspended by a strap

Fig. 54   Engraving by Albrecht Dürer (1471–1528)

held by a wild man who is making advances to the woman. The skull on the shield may be that of her husband and the mantling and her dress may represent her weeds. Albrecht Dürer's own armorial bearings dated 1523 are shown in *Fig. 55*; the shield is facing the sinister. Another artist of the same school who has drawn a ship under sail on the shield has interpreted the mantling not as acanthus leaves but as seaweed.

I have in my possesion two very unusual heraldic bookplates that originally belonged to Francis Martin, FSA, who was Bluemantle Pursuivant in 1797 before being promoted to Windsor Herald in 1819, then to Norroy King of Arms in 1839, and finally to Clarenceux King of Arms in 1846. As an alternative to the mantle or Robe of Estate, Martin made use of his herald's tabard upon which to place his arms. (His Pursuivant's tabard, with the electoral bonnet of 1801 altered to the crown of 1814, is in the London Museum.) On the bookplate his tabard is shown complete with side panels but omitting the royal arms on the centre

Fig. 55 (opposite) Albrecht Dürer's own armorial bearings

Fig. 56 (left) Engraving by Albrecht Dürer

panel where his shield is displayed encircled by his collar of SS (a gold chain, signifying authority, with links formed from the letter S). When Martin was promoted to Norroy King of Arms, he had the plate re-engraved to show his personal arms impaled with the official arms of his office and his personal crest was replaced by the crown of a King of Arms.

Fig. 57   Engraving by Albrecht Dürer

COLOUR PLATE SECTION

PLATE I

FURS Several variations of the furs most often used in heraldry are illustrated. See page 17 for detailed descriptions.

PLATE II

a THE SHIELD OF PEACE FOR THE BLACK PRINCE From the tomb of Edward, the Black Prince, in Canterbury Cathedral.

b SHIELD OF THE COLLEGE OF ARMS A royal corporation responsible for granting armorial bearings and exercising jurisdiction in heraldic matters.

c MOORCOCKS Used in the arms of Sir Thomas More.

d PELICAN IN HER PIETY Seen to be wounding herself in the breast and distilling drops of blood to nourish her young. This is a powerful symbol often used in ecclesiastical heraldry.

e CORBET A raven-like bird, seen in the armorial bearings of the family of this name.

f ARMS OF THE PAINTER-STAINERS' COMPANY One of the livery companies of the City of London.

g PRIVATE BADGE

h MARTLETS Imaginary footless birds used as a charge in heraldry. The cadency mark of a fourth son.

PLATE III

a AZURE BILLETTY A LION RAMPANT OR THE ARMS OF NASSAU, introduced into the royal arms of England by William III.

b LION RAMPANT REGARDANT ARGENT Looking backwards.

c AN EARLY FORM OF LION

d THE RED LION OF SCOTLAND Borne within a double tressure flory-counter-flory. The field is gold (or yellow) so the tongue and claws remain red.

e GULES THREE LIONS PASSANT GUARDANT The lions of England.

f PURPURE A LION RAMPANT ARGENT QUEUE FOURCHÉ The tail is forked and must be seen to be different to the position 'double-queued', where the lion has two tails.

g THE ARMS OF THE MAUDE FAMILY. Argent three bars gemelles sable over all a lion rampant gules charged upon the shoulder with a cross crosslet or fitchy.

PLATE IV

a MAUNCH The long-cuffed sleeve from a fashionable dress of the Middle Ages.

b TORCH The symbol of learning and achievement.

c FETTERLOCK An ancient form of 'D'-lock, used in the heraldic badge of the House of York, in conjunction with a falcon.

d STIRRUP Elaborate horse-trappings reflected the wealth and status of the rider, indicating chevalier rank. Borne by the family of Gifford among others.

e SCYTHE An old agricultural implement. The handle is known in some parts of England as the 'sned'. A scythe is borne by the family of Sneyd in their arms.

f TILTING LANCE Made from very light timber, reinforced with bindings, *c.* 1530.

g SPURS The symbol of knighthood. Also borne by the family of Spurrier, who made spurs.

h TUN A barrel, shown here in flames, used as a missile in early warfare. The canting coat of the Cheshire family of Emberton (embers – ashes; tun – barrel).

PLATE V

a CLARION A type of small portable organ with pipes and a stand.

b WATER-BOUGET This is a device for carrying water that has developed from two bladders on a yoke, an earlier version of the milkmaid's pails. There is a great variety of shapes used by artists for this long-established charge.

c BATTLE-AXE Used in all types of combat.

d CANNON Iron cannon were first cast in England in 1543. Prior to this date large guns were made from bronze and had been used in a crude form since the beginning of the fifteenth century.

e BEACON The 'fiery cresset' referred to by Shakespeare. Lines of beacons through the country warned of impending invasion or other major events.

f HAWK-LURE An imitation bird made from two wings of the quarry for which the hawk is being flown. It is used to retrieve the hawk after it has stooped and is swung around the falconer's head on the lure-line. Hawks are trained to return to the lure rather than the fist.

g GARB A wheatsheaf, from the French *gerbe*.

PLATE VI

a SUN IN SPLENDOUR Always shown with a human face and alternately straight and wavy rays issuing from the perimeter. When the moon is depicted, there are no rays and she is known to be 'in her complement'. The sun can also be blazoned as 'in his glory'.

b BUGLE-HORN Generally shown as a bull or cow's horn, garnished with bands of a different colour and suspended from a cord or ribbon tied in a knot of three loops. There are several very ancient horns extant which represent the authority of royal foresters. It is a popular charge used by families whose name is associated with hunting.

c BUCKLE Borne by the family of Pelham, it represents security whether on a sword-belt or a garter.

d STRAPS AND BUCKLES Borne by the family of Pelham.

e CATHERINE WHEEL The instrument of torture used in the martyrdom of St Catherine. Usually portrayed as a cartwheel with spikes on its rim.

f EAGLE RISING, WINGS DISPLAYED AND INVERTED Bird of prey, renowned for its watchfulness.

PLATE VII

a ESCALLOP SHELLS One of the most popular charges in heraldry, borne by many families including the Dacres. Inherited from pilgrims who wore a metal badge in their hats or on their cloaks to identify them and encourage hospitality.

b FLEUR-DE-LYS The national emblem of France, the lily is the symbol of the Blessed Virgin Mary and used in heraldry throughout the world.

c ESTOILLE This star usually has six pointed wavy rays and unlike the mullet is never pierced.

d ROSE An emblem, a symbol and a badge of England, also the cadency mark of seventh son. The heraldic rose, based on a dog-rose, has five open petals and five sepals, and is shown 'seeded' and 'barbed'. The centre is coloured yellow and the barbs between the petals are green. The Tudor Rose is a white rose within a red rose, sometimes shown on a stalk with two leaves when it must be described as such.

e MULLET A five-pointed star which may be pierced in the centre. If it is pierced, it could be blazoned as a spur rowel. Also the cadency mark of a third son.

f ESCARBUNCLE A star-shaped device of metal strips, originally attached to the face of a shield to strengthen it. When borne in threes and sixes, resembles snowflakes. Seen in the Bayeaux tapestry.

g FLEAM An instrument used particularly by veterinary surgeons. Similar to a 'cut-throat' razor, it had an open blade and a curved handle.

PLATE VIII

a PHEON The broad-headed metal tip of an arrow or a spear. It is always shown with the inside edges of the point scalloped. When they are smooth, the charge is known as a broad-arrow.

b KEYS Symbols of security and of liberation. The arms shown here are those of the See of Winchester, namely 'Gules two Keys indorsed in bend the uppermost Argent the other Or a Sword interposed between them in bend sinister of the second the pommel and hilt gold'.

c PORTCULLIS A latticework timber gate lowered and raised vertically in front of a castle entrance. A symbol of security, it is borne by the Dukes of Beaufort as their crest and is used by both Houses of Parliament, the City of Westminster, Somerset Herald and Portcullis Pursuivant. Since 1499 it is sometimes shown with a royal crown ensigning it.

d GRENADE This is a primitive exploding bomb fired from a cannon, from which the Grenadier Guards took their name. Also borne by several military families including the Cartwrights of Aynho.

e SPEARHEADS Argent three spearheads embrued with drops of blood, sable points upwards. The ancient arms of a noble tribe of North Wales. Nefydd Hardd, Lord of Nant Conway, founded the sixth Noble Tribe and bore these arms.

f SWORD The plain English broad-sword combines the symbols of authority and the cross of Christ. It must be one of the charges most used in heraldry. The parts of a sword that may be used are: the blade, which may be in pale, point upwards or reversed, or in bend and bend sinister; the guard, which terminates in quillons; and the pommel at the end of the grip. The metal protection at the end of the scabbard is known as the chape. A sword with gold hilt and pommel is the badge of the Dymoke family of Scivelsby, hereditary Champions to the Sovereign.

g TOWER This can be illustrated as a single tower or with a number of other small towers issuing from its battlements. It has a door known as a 'port', sometimes with a portcullis, and with arrow slits as windows. If the brickwork is portrayed in a different colour, it is blazoned as 'masoned' of another tincture. A popular device for the armorial bearings of towns, cities and private individuals who have devoted their lives to civic duties.

h SCALING LADDER Borne in the arms of military families who have achieved renown in the storming of a town or castle.

PLATE IX

a POT HELM The Crusader type of helm worn from the twelfth century onwards. This is still the type of helm favoured by Scottish heraldic artists.

b PAGEANT HELM This is always shown with a burnished silver steel finish and gilded bars. The lining is generally shown in red but this is not an invariable rule. It is used in heraldry by peers of the realm of the United Kingdom, and members of the nobility in Europe.

c TILTING HELM This is the helm used by gentlemen and esquires in heraldry and is made from steel. This example, known as the 'Brocas helm', was made in *c*. 1490, and is a fine existing piece of armour of the period.

d PRANKER HELM Made in Austria in *c*. 1350. The removable crest is a good example of the decorated buffalo horns so popular in Europe.

e GREAT HELM For the tilt in jousting, English, *c*. 1515.

f BARONET'S and KNIGHT'S HELM This is shown as a visored sixteenth-century close-helm affronté with the visor raised. The finish is burnished steel.

PLATE X

a CORONET OF A BARON A circlet of silver gilt upon which are seen four 'pearls' or silver balls. This coronet was assigned by Royal Warrant, by Charles II, to barons of England, and later by James II, to Barons of Ireland. The gilt rim encircles a crimson velvet cap, lined with and turned up ermine, topped with a tassel of gold bullion. A baron's coronet is the only one to have a plain rim with no embossed gemstones.

b CORONET OF A VISCOUNT This coronet has nine 'pearls' visible, and is otherwise similar to that of a baron. The rim is chased with jewels but not real stones, whereas the rim of a baron's coronet is plain. The rim is set around a velvet cap lined with and turned up ermine.

c CORONET OF AN EARL This is slightly different to the foregoing coronets as the five 'pearls' are raised upon points or spikes set on the rim between four strawberry leaves.

d CELESTIAL CROWN Similar to an Eastern crown with each point tipped with a star. Used by persons and companies connected with flying.

e CORONET OF A MARQUESS This is a rim of silver gilt set with 'pearls' and strawberry leaves. In heraldic representations, two 'pearls' are visible between three strawberry leaves. The chasing on the rim and the velvet cap lined with ermine are similar to the previous examples of coronets of rank.

f CORONET OF A DUKE This shows five strawberry leaves set upon a silver gilt circlet chased with precious stones. Real gems are only used in the royal crowns. The rim encloses a cap of crimson velvet turned up ermine with a gold bullion tassel at the top.

g EASTERN CROWN A circlet with five triangular points used by families and corporate bodies connected with the Eastern hemisphere, for example Brooke, the White Rajah of Sarawak, whose arms were ensigned by an Eastern Crown and bore as his Badge an Eastern Crown within an annulet with the name Sarawak.

h CHAPLET This is not really a coronet but a wreath and it comes in several forms. It is made up from oak-leaves and acorns, or just oak-leaves, and sometimes laurel, and usually has four flowers. It was the victor's crown in ancient times and Napoleon had one made for himself in gold.

i ARMS OF H.M. THE QUEEN, and THE UNITED KINGDOM Showing the heraldic representation of St. Edward's Crown and the gilded helm of the royal family.

j MURAL CROWN Generally borne by civic authorities and towns as it represents a city wall.

k ARMS OF H. M. THE QUEEN AS USED IN SCOTLAND Showing the flag of St Andrew and the flag of St George. The lion on top of the crown is shown in a different position to the English lion.

l NAVAL CROWN This was very popular after the Napoleonic Wars when many English admirals and captains were granted armorial bearings, or had their existing arms augmented in recognition of their bravery and

PLATE I

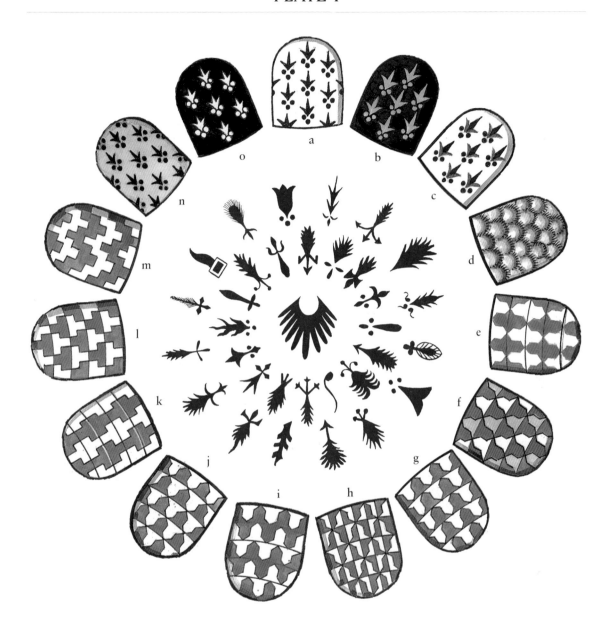

a	Ermine	i	Vair en point
b	Pean	j	Vair
c	Erminites	k	Counter-potent
d	Natural	l	Potent
e	Counter-Vair	m	Potent-counter-
f	Vair of four		potent
	tinctures	n	Erminois
g	Vair in pale	o	Ermines
h	Alternate Vair		

PLATE II

a The Shield of Peace for the Black Prince

b Shield of the College of Arms

c Moorcocks   d Pelican in her piety   e Corbet

f Arms of the Painter-Stainers' Company   g Private badge   h Martlets

PLATE IV

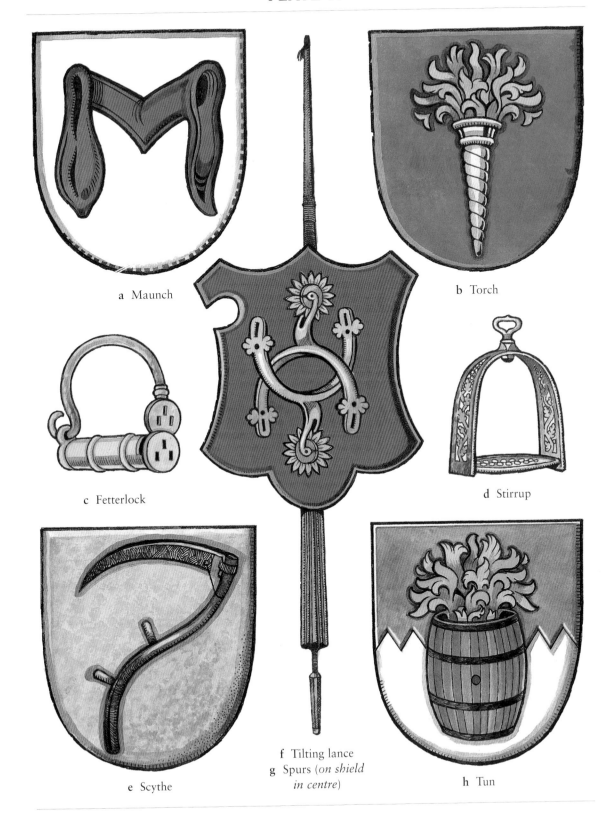

a Maunch

b Torch

c Fetterlock

d Stirrup

e Scythe

f Tilting lance
g Spurs (*on shield in centre*)

h Tun

PLATE III

a Azure billetty a lion rampant or

b Lion rampant regardant Argent

c An early form of lion

d The red lion
of Scotland

e Gules three lions passant guardant

f Purpure a lion rampant Argent queue fourché

g The arms of the Maude family

PLATE V

a Clarion

b Water-bouget

c Battle-axe

d Cannon

e Beacon

f Hawk-lure

g Garb

PLATE VI

a Sun in splen-

b Bugle-horn

d

d

c (*centre*) Buckle
d (*either side*)
Straps and buckles

e Catherine wheel

f Eagle rising

PLATE VII

a Escallop shells

b Fleur-de-lys

c Estoille

d Rose

e Mullet

f Escarbuncle

g Fleam

PLATE VIII

a Pheon

b Keys

c Portcullis

d Grenade

e Spearheads

f Sword
g Tower (*on
shield in centre*)

h Scaling ladder

PLATE IX

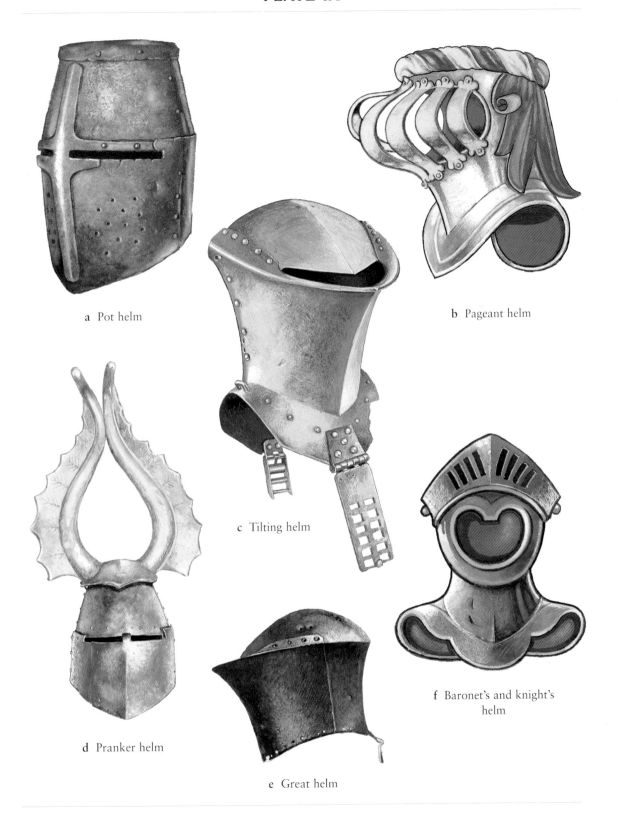

a Pot helm

b Pageant helm

c Tilting helm

d Pranker helm

e Great helm

f Baronet's and knight's
helm

PLATE X

a Coronet of a baron

b Coronet of a viscount

c Coronet of an earl

d Celestial crown

e Coronet of a marquess

f Coronet of a duke

g Eastern crown

i Arms of H.M. the Queen and the
United Kingdom

h Chaplet

j Mural crown

k Arms of H.M. the Queen as used
in Scotland

l Naval crown

m Cap of Estate
(or Cap of Maintenance)

n Crest coronet
(or ducal coronet)

o Vallary crown

p Coronet of Prince
of Wales

q Crown of King of Arms

r Foreign crown,
Kingdom of Hanover

PLATE XI

a A complicated
eighteenth-century form
of mantling

c The Garter stall-plate of Ralph,
Lord Basset of Drayton (c. 1368)

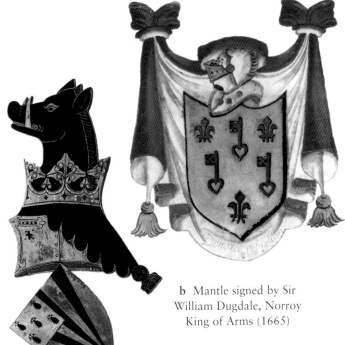

b Mantle signed by Sir
William Dugdale, Norroy
King of Arms (1665)

d Contemporary form of mantling with
gentleman's helm

e Contemporary form of mantling showing helm
used by baronets and knights

PLATE XII

a Helm and mantling

b Lymphad

c Open book

d Anchor

e The ancient arms of France

f Male-griffin crest

g Fleur-de-lys

PLATE XIII

a Dragon

b Wyvern

c Dragon's head

d Amphitère

e Boreyne

f Cockatrice

g Hydra

PLATE XIV

a Griffin

b Angel

c Serpent-woman

d Opinicus

e Winged woman

f Pegasus

g Winged bull

PLATE XV

a Musimon

b Heraldic panther

c Heraldic tyger

d Yale

e Heraldic antelope

PLATE XVI

a Eagle displayed

b Unicorn passant

c Eagle's leg à la quise

d Unicorn from the *Mappa Mundi*

e The unicorn and maiden

f Boar's head couped close

g A unicorn salient

h Eagle rising

success. The rim of the circlet is decorated with the sterns of three warships, between which are two square sails. The equivalent for the mercantile service is a rim set with five sails. The crown or coronet may be of any colour and in several examples the name of an action where the recipient gained honour is inscribed upon the circlet.

m CAP OF ESTATE or CAP OF MAINTENANCE (sometimes called a chapeau). This ancient piece of headgear is sometimes seen instead of a crest wreath, which implies an element of distinction and antiquity to the coat of arms.

n CREST CORONET or DUCAL CORONET This is a small coronet showing three strawberry leaves set upon a rim of any colour. It does not imply title or noble status, and has no precedence over any other crest. Nevertheless it has always been popular in Europe where the rules of heraldry and armory have not been held so tightly in rein as they are in the United Kingdom. The crest coronet is however seen widely in English heraldry and it must have been a useful alternative to the crest wreath when actual crests were being laced on to tilting helms.

o VALLARY CROWN A circlet set with five pieces shaped roughly like the fur Vair. This could reflect the squirrel skins of Vair, or it might reflect the spaces between the uprights as valleys.

p CORONET OF THE PRINCE OF WALES Designed by Louis Osman for the Investiture of the Prince of Wales in Caernarvon Castle on 1 July 1969. It has only one arch, whereas royal crowns have two. This symbolic diadem is the latest item of regalia to enter the Crown Jewels.

q CROWN OF KINGS OF ARMS The only people other than royalty and peers of the realm permitted to wear and display crowns are the Kings of Arms. The crown has sixteen acanthus leaves set upon the rim, of which nine appear in heraldic representations. Instead of embossed gemstones, part of the first verse of Psalm LI is worked into the rim, namely '*Miserere mei Deus* [apparent] *secundum magnam misericordiam tuam*'.

r FOREIGN CROWN The crown of the Kingdom of Hanover as used in the British Royal Arms from 1816 to 1837.

PLATE XI

a A complicated form of mantling popular from the seventeenth century to the nineteenth century.

b A very simple mantle, almost in the form of a robe of estate, dated 1665 and signed by Sir William Dugdale, Norroy King of Arms. The painting would have been completed some time after this date, when the heralds had returned to London from their 'Visitation of Yorkshire'.

c An early form of mantling seen on the Garter stall-plate of Ralph, Lord Basset of Drayton, in St George's Chapel, Windsor Castle (*c.* 1368). The mantling appears to be a continuation of the boar's body.

d The style of mantling in current use, although no rules have ever existed concerning artistic representation and a person entitled to arms may choose whatever form they desire.

e The current form of mantling shown with the helm of a knight or a baronet, with the visor raised.

PLATE XII

a HELM AND MANTLING of a gentleman or an esquire shown in 'trian-aspect' or three-quarter profile with the crest on the same axis.

b LYMPHAD An ancient ship or galley with one or three masts. The sails are generally shown furled, with pennants flying from the mast-tops.

c OPEN BOOK This is a popular Charge for academic bodies and should be described in detail in the blazon. The edges of the pages and the clasps may be gold and the colour of the binding should be stated. It is assumed that the pages are white and the printing or writing black.

d ANCHOR The common anchor has five main parts; the shank, the stock, the ring, the arms and the flukes. These parts may be shown in different colours or in their natural colours when the anchor is blazoned 'proper'. It is always shown in a vertical position unless described otherwise, e.g. the flag of the Lord High Admiral of the United Kingdom displays an anchor fesswise. A rope or cable is often attached to the ring. The anchor is a symbol of hope.

e THE ANCIENT ARMS OF FRANCE A blue field semé (powdered or scattered with) golden fleurs-de-lys.

f MALE GRIFFIN CREST Clearly showing the tufts or spikes issuing from its body, and the absence of wings, which distinguishes it from an ordinary Griffin.

g FLEUR-DE-LYS The royal badge of France. In its stylized heraldic form it represents a lily, which is one of the symbols of the Virgin Mary and stands for purity. It was adopted by King Louis VII of France as a royal device in the twelfth century and was quartered with the royal arms of England from the time of Edward III until 1801. The ancient coat of France scattered with gold lilies on a blue field was originally borne with the English lions, but the number was reduced to three fleur-de-lys in around 1411.

PLATE XIII

a DRAGON A fabulous monster which has become the heraldic badge of Wales. St George and the Dragon appear both in England and in Russia.

b WYVERN A winged serpent-like dragon that was the emblem of the ancient kingdom of Wessex.

c DRAGON'S HEAD Seen here as a crest.

d AMPHITÈRE A winged serpent with a barbed tail.

e BOREYNE A small fictitious Tudor animal with ram's horns, a spined fin on its back and a barbed tongue.

f COCKATRICE Half cock and half serpent. Said to be hatched from the egg of a nine-year-old cock, by a toad on a dunghill. If the tail terminates in a dragon's head, the monster is termed a basilisk.

g HYDRA A many-headed (usually seven) monster killed by Hercules as his second labour to atone for killing his family. Seldom seen in heraldry but included in several reference books.

PLATE XIV

a GRIFFIN (Gryphon) A monster of great antiquity found in many countries throughout the world. Very popular in heraldry representing guardianship. The upper half is that of an eagle with large ears and a beard, and the lower half is that of a lion.

b ANGEL Celestial beings are included here as they are mythical and appear in heraldry. They are part human and part bird.

c SERPENT-WOMAN Seldom found in heraldry except in reference books.

d OPINICUS A handsome winged creature with the body of a lion, and the head and wings of an eagle.

e WINGED WOMAN Used as a crest in Germany. Probably not related to an angel.

f PEGASUS The winged horse born from the blood of Medusa after she had been killed by Perseus. Pegasus was ridden by Bellerophon, son of the king of Corinth, who tried to reach heaven itself on the horse's back, but without success.

g WINGED BULL The winged bull or ox is the symbol of St Luke, one of the four evangelists.

PLATE XV

a MUSIMON A goat-like creature with two sets of horns, one straight and the other curved.

b HERALDIC PANTHER Always shown covered with coloured spots, and issuing fire from its mouth and ears.

c HERALDIC TYGER A wolf-like animal with tusks and a spike at the end of its nose. The legend of the tyger is told on page 86.

d YALE A slender buffalo with tusks and long curved horns that swivel so that an adversary is always under attack regardless of which direction they come from. Two yales were used by Lady Margaret Beaufort as heraldic supporters. She became the mother of Henry VII, and the yale is now counted among the 'Queen's Beasts'.

e HERALDIC ANTELOPE This is distinguished from a natural antelope by its long serrated horns, its mane and the spike at the end of its nose.

PLATE XVI

a EAGLE DISPLAYED Shown in one of the many positions the bird can take in heraldry, and in this case the most satisfying aesthetically as it fits the shape of the shield to perfection.

b UNICORN PASSANT This is a slender horse-like creature with a flowing mane and a single horn issuing from its forehead.

c EAGLE'S LEG À LA QUISE The badge of the Stanley family, Earls of Derby.

d UNICORN Taken from the *Mappa Mundi* in Hereford Cathedral.

e THE UNICORN AND MAIDEN The legend is mentioned on page 88.

f BOAR'S HEAD COUPED CLOSE Shown in the Scottish manner, which differs from the English, as described on page 73.

g UNICORN SALIENT From the Latin *salire*, meaning to leap or jump.

h EAGLE RISING Another of the many positions in which the bird can be seen in heraldry.

BEASTS AND MONSTERS

THE criteria for inclusion in this section is that the beast or monster must have been described in some heraldic work, regardless of whether or not it has been seen on a shield or crest. Some of the monsters described on pages 82–104 and illustrated in *Plates XIII, XIV, XV* and *XVI* have never before been depicted; even so, the list does not pretend to be a complete record.

There is a very thin dividing line between some beasts and monsters; for example, the apres (*Fig. 93, page 83*) is a bull but with the tail of a bear (it appears as an heraldic device albeit on only one occasion). The heraldic definition of a beast is a representation of a natural animal, fish or insect, whereas a monster is either a combination of parts of other animals or an entirely fictitious creature.

These combinations are referred to as chimerical monsters after Chimera in Greek mythology, the offspring of Typhon and Echidna, which was composed of the forequarters of a lion, the middle parts of a she-goat and the tail of a snake. The chimera (*Fig. 99, page 85*) is generally depicted with three heads breathing fire. The usual characteristics of these monsters are aggression, vigilance and defiance. The Bible tells us of the cockatrice, illustrated in *Plate XIII*, and the mandrake (*Fig. 116, page 92*), in addition to the celestial beings of the angels which, according to our definition, are monsters of partly human and partly bird form.

The beasts and monsters shown in this section are drawn from the imagination of heralds and artists, some ancient and some comparatively modern. The older beasts are mainly of Asian or Mediterranean origin and it can be readily understood that the tales of travellers and crusaders found their way in graphic form into the bestiaries of the medieval period that were meant to put the fear of God into miscreants. Some of the descriptions and memories were inevitably confused and must have seemed wholly incredible to the desk-bound scholars who had remained at home. These tales, combined with the documentary evidence which the scholars possessed, such as the world map made in 1300, the *Mappa Mundi* in Hereford Cathedral, showing all kinds of fabulous beasts, compounded the images of monsters almost beyond people's wildest dreams (see *Plate XVI*).

In the recondite world of the medieval bestiaries there are many fabulous creatures that are rarely seen even in heraldry. These fictitious animal concoctions provide a degree of entertainment today that was totally lacking at their conception. The intention of the creators of most of the monsters was to frighten an uneducated and gullible population, consisting mainly of agricultural labourers, into the ways of morality, Christianity and personal discipline. The mother's threat to her child that 'the bogey-man will get you' was intermingled with crusaders' half-remembered tales of lions and vultures and elaborated on by Christian scholars to compile a terrifying collection of monsters. The illiterate public did not dare to question the validity of the existence of such creatures as they were often given certain provenance by the scholars speaking of countries far beyond the imagination of an English villager.

It must be remembered that the world in the Middle Ages was mysterious, its lands unexplored, its seas unfathomed, its forests haunted by unpredictable forces and its nights sinister with malevolent darkness. The uneducated labourers of the field must have regarded the world with a mixture of fear and blind faith, curiosity and credulity, suspicion and superstition. They acquired what little knowledge they had from ecclesiastical stained glass, wall-paintings and sculpture. The privileged few, such as the land-owning feudal nobility and the clergy, who had access to books, would have had enough formal education to appreciate the artistry of the bestiaries and to relish the grotesque creatures. They would however have been totally unable either to prove or disprove what they saw and read.

The village priest, who was also the local scholar, would never have seen a crocodile in his life but he would have heard about dragons in his studies and he would have known about the cockatrice from the Bible. One can scarcely imagine the impact made by a traveller's marvellous accounts of lions, vultures, camels, giraffes and creatures for which he had no name, on his fellow countrymen who only knew horses, cows, dogs and the beasts of their own land. People of those days were much closer to the earth than we are now but their ability to put two and two together must not be underestimated. Cross-breeding was understood with horses, mules, asses and so forth, so the integrity of a traveller who claimed to have seen a spotted camel with a long neck and curved horns was not doubted.

The principal stable of horrors, however, owes its origin to the fecund imagination of the Tudor heralds who built upon the medieval foundations and added many fantastic beasts which now seem to us, in this more enlightened age, almost endearing. It is hard for us to imagine why Sir Thomas Cheyney, a Knight of the Garter in the reign of Henry VIII, should have requested a theow or thos as the supporter of his banner, but if he had happened at the time to have had a favourite small dog, the heralds might have suggested that it was given hooves to convert it into a chimerical creature resembling the monster in the ancient bestiaries. In this way heraldry developed and as the Kings of Arms were in control, they allowed imaginative beasts and monsters to come into existence, provided that they were distinctive and properly placed on official record at the College of Arms.

It is a source of amusement now to identify the different animals that are amalgamated in some of the most eccentric creatures. One feels that the Tudor heralds in desperation threw the parts of many animals into a melting pot to see what emerged. Nevertheless, the results have given English heraldry a feast of wonderful and improbable creatures which have entertained and amused us for five hundred years. There is, however, a possibility, which must not be overlooked, that these monsters were created with deadly seriousness and were intended to inspire awe and respect from the lesser non-armigerous mortals.

When beasts and monsters are mentioned in a blazon, their attitude must be properly described. The illustrations in this book show most of the principal positions that relate to all animals in heraldry. One or two descriptions relate only to certain beasts and monsters: a horse is never rampant but is called 'forcene' when rearing on its hind legs; a griffin is said to be 'segreant' when standing upright with its wings together; and a silver lion with a forked tail looking backwards, on a purple shield, is blazoned 'Purpure a lion regardant queue-fourché Argent'.

Fig. 58   Ape or monkey

Fig. 59a   Badger (or Brock)

Fig. 59b   Badger masks

BEASTS

Beasts have featured prominently in heraldry from the earliest times. In many countries man has tended to represent himself in the image of a wild beast to boast of his prowess and to boost his ego. First and foremost, the lion has been used in heraldry since the twelfth century when Geoffrey Plantagenet, Count of Anjou, bore on his shield rampant lions which can be seen on his tomb, now in the museum at Le Mans. He died in 1150, which means that his heraldic shield is probably the earliest in existence.

Any kind of animal can be portrayed in heraldry and most have been at some time or another. The following list includes the most popular beasts.

APE OR MONKEY *(Fig. 58)* The monkey is seldom encountered but the arms of the family of Carter of Eccleshall Castle in Staffordshire display a demi-monkey issuing from the battlement of a tower. When an ape or a monkey is collared and chained, the collar is usually shown around the animal's waist.

ASS *(Fig. 60)* Borne from ancient times by the family of Cavenagh-Mainwaring of Whitmore Hall in Staffordshire. The beast's head issues from a crest coronet.

BADGER *(Fig. 59)* This is to be found in a number of English coats of arms and reflects both country life and the similarity of its old name 'Brock' to a number of surnames. Brocklehurst, Brocklebank and Brooke are examples.

Fig. 60   Ass

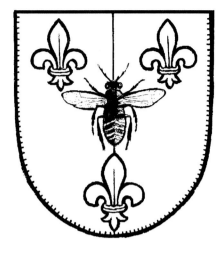

Fig. 62   Bee

Fig. 61   Bear

BEAR *(Fig. 61)* The best-known example of the bear in English heraldry is the device of the Earls of Warwick who display a bear and ragged staff. Other families such as Baring and Barwick also employ bears in their arms.

BEE *(Fig. 62)* The symbol of industry, the bee appears in the arms of Manchester and various other northern towns in England and in the arms of successful industrialists.

BENGAL TIGER *(Fig. 63)* This is a natural tiger and not to be confused with the heraldic tyger. A Bengal tiger couchant was borne by the late Rodney Dennys, Somerset Herald of Arms, as his crest.

Fig. 63   Bengal tiger

BOAR *(Fig. 64)* The sanglier is met with frequently in British and European heraldry and is another animal that reflects the hunting instincts of our ancestors. This is not the domestic pig but the wild boar that still exists in the forests of the Continent. The wild boar is to be found most often in the heraldry of Scotland where it has its own peculiar manner of being shown. In England a boar's head is generally shown erased, with tufts of hair descending from the neck which is in a vertical position. In Scotland the head is shown 'couped close' (that is, with no neck, and chopped off close behind the ears). A good 'canting' crest (that is a visual pun on a name) is to be found in the crest of Swinton.

Fig. 64   Boar's head

Fig. 65   Bull's head caboshed

Fig. 66   Camel

Fig. 67   Wild cat or cat-a-mountain

BULL *(Fig. 65)* This animal sometimes appears in heraldry and usually as a supporter to the shield. The Marquess of Abergavenny bears a bull as his crest and pied bulls as his supporters. The City of Oxford has a canting coat showing an ox walking through water. The bull's head is also found caboshed. Calves are to be found in the ancient coat of the family of Calvely from Cheshire, where there is an alabaster monument in Bunbury church.

CAMEL *(Fig. 66)* This animal is met with most frequently in the arms of companies who trade in the East. The Worshipful Company of Grocers in the City of London has as its crest 'a Camel passant Or bridled Sable on his back a bale Argent charged with six cloves Sable and corded of the last'. Lord Kitchener has a camel as one of his supporters.

CAT *(Fig. 67)* This domestic creature is occasionally found in heraldry and care must be taken in distinguishing it from lions and leopards. The family of Adams bears three domestic cats in its arms, but the more ferocious kind which is known as a cat-a-mountain is found in the arms of the families of Keats and Scott-Gatty.

CROCODILE *(Fig. 68)* This animal appears in the arms of Speke and also in the arms of Westcar. The crocodile is the principal charge in the armorial bearings of Lesotho, being the emblem of the ruling dynasty.

Fig. 68   Crocodile

ELEPHANT *(Fig. 69)* This is found frequently in heraldry and the best-known example is the Elephant and Castle, which has given its name to a district of London as well as many public houses. There is a theory that the term originates from an incorrect reading of the Infanta of Castille, but this is not proved. The elephant features in the arms of Sutcliffe and Elliott.

FISH *(Fig. 70)* Fish are popular creatures in heraldry and usually take the form of the dolphin which is associated with many seafaring families and also seaside towns. Giles de Fishbourn bore 'Gules a Dolphin naiant embowed argent' in the time of Henry III. 'Naiant' means swimming, 'urinant' means diving and 'hauriant' means pointing upwards. The eldest son of the King of France was known as the Dauphin, and the arches on his coronet were fashioned in the form of dolphins. Pike, which are known in heraldry as lucies, have been borne by the Lucy family for many years. The family of Gascoyne bears a demi-luce (Heralds' Visitation 1612) which is sometimes blazoned as the head of an eel. The City of Glasgow has a salmon in its arms.

FOX *(Fig. 71)* The arms of the baronetcy of Williams-Wynn bear two foxes salient crossed in saltire, which can be seen on public-house signs in North Wales, giving rise to the incorrect slogan of the 'cross foxes'.

GOAT *(Fig. 72)* This animal is often found in English heraldry, the best-known example being the supporters of the Lord Bagot whose family have kept a herd of rare goats on their estate in Staffordshire for hundreds of years.

Fig. 69   Elephant and castle

Fig. 70   Fish

Fig. 72   Goat

Fig. 71   Crossed foxes

Fig. 73   Greyhound

Fig. 75   Hedgehog

Fig. 76   Horse

GREYHOUND *(Fig. 73)* This dog does not feature quite so frequently as the Talbot but can be seen in the arms of Hunter and Clayhills.

HARE *(Fig. 74)* Seldom met with in heraldry, the hare is surrounded by legend and superstition. The hare in conjunction with sporting items has been granted recently to a hunt in the Midlands of England. Many marvellous and mysterious faculties, even to the point of witchcraft, are attributed by countrymen to the hare. Any person who has observed the antics of the mad March hare will readily believe almost anything that is written about this engaging creature.

The picture of a hare playing upon the bagpipes is going almost too far, yet it is to be seen in the arms of Hopwell, of Hopwell in Derbyshire.

A French manuscript illustrates a country peasant, an average agricultural labourer, playing the bagpipes, of which the bag or bladder is made from the skin of a hare and the chanter pipe is issuing from the mouth of the animal. This might possibly account for the English legend of the hare actually playing the instrument.

The hare is described in some books as a cony (rabbit). Rabbits and hares appear in heraldry from medieval times, and one delightful device shows three conies 'trijunct' sharing three ears. This charge is illustrated in Randle Holme's book and is attributed to Harry Well.

The hare, together with many other beasts, has been given wings by the heralds although it needs none to escape its pursuers. A winged hare was granted to Arthur James Hare, in 1923.

A hare's scalp with ears erect proper is the crest of the Dymoke family, the eldest of which is the Honourable the Queen's Champion by hereditary right.

HEDGEHOG *(Fig. 75)* This creature is known in heraldry as an 'urchin' or 'Urcheon', which reminds us that the sea-urchin also has spines. The family of Harris bears a hedgehog which is known in French as an *hérisson*.

HORSE *(Fig. 76)* This is a popular beast in heraldry especially as a supporter but the best-known horse must be the white horse of Hanover, or Westphalia, which was borne in the royal arms of England. The family of Lane of King's Bromley bear a demi-horse as their crest to commemorate the heroic act of Jane Lane in assisting King Charles II to escape after the battle of Worcester.

Fig. 74
a Natural hare
b Hares tricorporate
c Hare playing the bagpipes
d Peasant, from French medieval
manuscript

Fig. 77a   Grasshopper

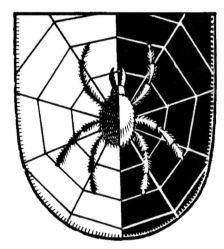

Fig. 77b   Spider in web

Fig. 78   Natural leopard

INSECTS *(Fig. 77)* Grasshoppers, spiders and other insects are to be found in heraldry from time to time, specifically in the arms of Gresham and Webb. The family of Kendiffe bears an ant in its arms.

LEOPARD *(Fig. 78)* This animal is unusual in British heraldry and generally appears as a crest. It springs from the same family as heraldic lions and lioncels. *Pardus* is Latin for panther, and the word 'pard' generally refers to an animal with a spotted coat (hence Camelopardel for giraffe).

LION *(Fig. 79)* As a symbol of majesty and superiority the lion can be displayed in many different positions, standing on its hind leg (rampant) or on four legs (passant), looking straight ahead (affronté), or looking out at the observer (guardant).

Fig. 79   Lion's face

It can be shown looking over its shoulder (regardant) and with one or two tails. It can be dormant and even cowardly with its tail between its legs. In fact the permutations are almost endless and it is interesting that arms with lions in new positions and in new colour combinations are still being granted by the Kings of Arms today after seven hundred years. A crowned lion's head affronté is illustrated on a banner.

LYNX *(Fig. 80)* An infrequent visitor to British heraldry but it is to be found as the crest of Lynch. It was believed to have such sharp eyesight that it could see through walls.

MOLE *(Fig. 81)* This creature is possibly the origin of furs used in heraldry. The moldiwarp, or want, as it is sometimes called, is borne in the arms of Mitford and in the arms of Sir Ranulph Twisleton-Wykeham-Fiennes, the explorer, who bears Argent a Chevron between three moles Sable, for Twisleton.

PORCUPINE *(Fig. 82)* This unusual beast was used by Lord De L'Isle, Simon Eyre, Lord Mayor of London in 1445, and in a recent grant where the porcupine is shown reading a book.

RABBIT *(Fig. 83)* Known in heraldry as a cony, it appears in the arms of Coningsby and Montgomery Cunningham. It also gives its name to many English place names such as Coneyhurst in Sussex.

Fig. 80   Lynx

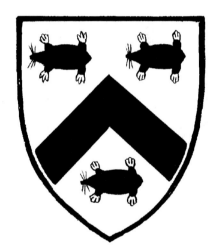

Fig. 81   Moles

Fig. 83   Rabbit

Fig. 82   Porcupine

Fig. 84a   Ram

Fig. 84b   Pascal lamb

Fig. 85   Rhinoceros

RAMS AND SHEEP *(Fig. 84)* A sheep is seen more often than a ram in heraldry because of the Christian symbol of the Pascal lamb which has always been a popular charge and is to be seen on the sign of many public houses called the Lamb and Flag. The other representation of the lamb or sheep is in the Spanish Order of Chivalry called the Golden Fleece, the Spanish equivalent to the English Order of the Garter. The fleece appears frequently in the arms of towns whose staple is wool.

RHINOCEROS *(Fig. 85)* Known to the ancients for the efficacious use of its horn when ground to a powder, the rhinoceros is borne as a crest by the Worshipful Company of Apothecaries and may be seen over the gates of the Physic Garden in Chelsea.

SQUIRREL *(Fig. 86)* This is always shown as a red squirrel and is usually holding and eating a nut.

STAG *(Fig. 87)* There are many kinds of deer, male and female, but they are usually referred to as a stag. This animal has its own special terms for denoting its heraldic position on a shield, and the old terms of venery still persist. Hence a stag will be 'lodged' if lying down and 'trippant' if running. When it is looking out of the shield at the observer, it is termed 'at gaze'. The antlers of a stag are called 'attires' and each tyne

Fig. 86   Squirrel

Fig. 87b   Stag's head caboshed

Fig. 87a   Stag

or branch has a separate name. The stag as the principal beast of the chase obviously reflects the sport of hunting for the gentry. Private estates would have had a deer park, so a stag is a natural choice of beast for a country landowner. The deer's head is sometimes shown caboshed and sometimes erased. The noble families of Cavendish, Dukes of Devonshire, and the Stanleys, Earls of Derby, both feature stags in their arms.

Fig. 88   Talbot

TALBOT *(Fig. 88)* Much has been written about the development of the hunting dogs or hounds of England and it seems that the Talbot was a type of bloodhound known as the Barlow's Southern-mouthed Hound. It was definitely a hound of the chase which hunted by scent, and not a 'gazehound' like a greyhound which pursues its quarry by sight. The Talbot was a heavy dog with long ears and heavy dewlaps. Its underlining was deep and its general appearance sturdy. The Talbot can be seen in the arms of the Earls of Shrewsbury and of the Wolseley family.

WOLF *(Fig. 89)* This beast is frequently met with in armory and reflects the distant past when wolves roamed the forests of Europe.

Fig. 89   Wolf

Fig. 90   Alce

Fig. 91   Allocamellus

Fig. 92   Alphyn

MONSTERS

QUADRUPED

ALCE *(Fig. 90)* A large deer-like animal somewhat like an elk, supposedly from Germany. The alce is not found in English armory, apart from its inclusion in dictionaries on the subject and a mention in the writings of Julius Caesar. It apparently had no joints in its legs so in order to catch it, hunters would saw halfway through the tree that it leant against to sleep; when the tree broke, the alce could be picked up and carried away.

ALLOCAMELLUS *(Fig. 91)* A little-known and ugly creature sometimes referred to as an ass-camel. The only known instance of its use is in the arms of the East Land Company which existed in Elizabethan times. Unfortunately the company's arms were not recorded at the College of Arms so there is no way of establishing this curious monster in the mythical zoo. One can only suppose that the combination of two beasts of burden was meant to signify mutual effort. But who was the camel, and who was the ass? The company did not survive, nor did the allocamellus.

ALPHYN or ALFYN *(Fig. 92)* A quadruped somewhat like an heraldic tyger but having the forelegs and talons of an eagle. The creature has a knotted tail, long ears, a mane and tufts of hair which spring from all parts of its body. The heraldic badge of Richard West, the seventh Lord de la Warr, and also found on the Garter stall-plate of Sir William Chamberlain (1461).

APRES *(Fig. 93)* A curious concoction of bull and bear of Russian origin, the apres only appears in the coat of arms of the Worshipful Company and Fellowship of the Merchant Adventurers trading to Muscovia, commonly called the Company of Muscovy or Russian Merchants. The apres has the body and head of a bull with the tail of a bear, symbolizing strength. Could this creature possibly be a yak?

BAGWYN *(Fig. 94)* This is another beast of the stag or antelope kind with cloven hooves, antlers and a bushy tail. The first appearance of the bagwyn is in *Prince Arthur's Book* (c. 1539), where it supports the banner of the Earl of Arundel. The Earl's son Henry, who became a Knight of the Garter and godson of Henry VIII, used a bagwyn as the sinister supporter of his coat of arms which may be seen in St George's Chapel, Windsor, on his Garter stall-plate.

BONACON *(Fig. 95)* A bull-like animal with small horns curled in like a ram's, a horse's tail and a mane. This beast was known to Aristotle and Pliny and also makes its presence known in the *Mappa Mundi* in Hereford Cathedral. It is difficult to understand why anyone should want a bonacon to feature prominently in their arms as the creature's only real claim to fame lies in the manner in which it defends itself. Upon being pursued, it raises its tail and emits such a noxious gas that trees within three acres catch fire. Naturally the enthusiasm of any pursuer would be dampened by this powerful emission. Only the bonacon's head is seen in English heraldry. In 1560, a bonacon's head was granted to Richard Candelor of Walsingham in Norfolk, and in the following year a grant was made to Hugh Hollynside of Cheshire.

BOREYNE (see *Plate XIII)* This is an extraordinary dog-like monster with huge claws, a mane, curved horns, a pointed tongue and a webbed fin running along its back. It only appears as the heraldic device of Sir Thomas Borough (or Burgh), K.G., in the late fifteenth century.

CALOPUS *(Fig. 96)* Also known as a caleps chatloup and catwolf, this is another creature of whom only one exists, and that is in the records of the College of Arms. Godfrey Foljambe of Walton in Derbyshire was granted a calopus in

Fig. 93   Apres

Fig. 94   Bagwyn

Fig. 96   Calopus

Fig. 95   Bonacon

a   b   c

Fig. 97
a Calygreyhound
b Caretyne
c Theow

1513, by Thomas Wriothesley, Garter King of Arms, for use on his heraldic standard. The imaginary animal has the body of a wolf, the head of a cat and a pair of serrated horns.

CALYGREYHOUND *(Fig. 97a)* A small dog-like creature with a long thin tufted tail, the forelegs of a bird of prey and antlers which take the form of oak-leaves. The calygreyhound was the heraldic badge of John de Vere, Earl of Oxford, who used this creature on his seal. He was executed in 1462 so the animal existed in armory prior to that date. His son, another John, was very fond of his badge and used the calygreyhound on his silver, church plate, tapestries and wall-hangings.

CARETYNE *(Fig. 97b)* This is another Tudor invention which did not breed as there seems to be only one example of it, and that is in a book of heraldic badges at the College of Arms. Sir Francis Bacon, the Tudor courtier and poet, bore as his badge a caretyne which is a cloven-hoofed quadruped with a long tail, tufts of hair issuing from its body, tusks and breathing fire.

THEOW *(Fig. 97c)* This is a fifteenth-century invention based upon the jackal, but instead of paws, it is shown with hooves. A theow supports the banner of the Tudor courtier, Sir Thomas Cheyney, K. G., in *Prince Arthur's Book*.

CAMELOPARDEL *(Fig. 98)* This creature looks like a giraffe (camelopard) with the addition of two long curved horns reaching over its back. The word camelopardel means camel

Fig. 98　Camelopardel

combined with 'pard' meaning spotted skin (i.e. leopard = a lion with a spotted skin). The camelopard, the allocamelus and the camelopardel are all basically giraffes with minor variations. The giraffe must have been seen by early travellers who did not have a name for such an animal, hence their invention of 'spotted camel'.

CHIMERA *(Fig. 99)* An imaginary beast of ancient origin invented by the Greeks. The chimera comes from a mountain in Lycia which was volcanic. Lions lived close to the top, goats lived in the middle region, and snakes dwelt at its foot. The Chimera in Greek mythology was destroyed by Bellerophon who flew over it on Pegasus and shot it with his arrows. The chimera had the body, head, mane and legs of a lion with a goat's head issuing from its back, and the tail of a dragon or serpent. Several variations of the chimera exist and it has given its name to all chimerical beasts of fabulous invention. It is not seen in English heraldry. It breathes fire and might also have the head of a dragon.

Fig. 99   Chimera

EGRENTYNE *(Fig. 100)* A dog-like creature that had webbed hind feet, cloven hooves on the forelegs and a long straight tail with three tufts. The only egrentyne in existence was granted to Sir John Falstofe, K.G., in the sixteenth century as an heraldic supporter.

ENFIELD *(Fig. 101)* This is another composite beast with the head and ears of a fox, the body of a wolf and the forelegs of an eagle. It is seen in the arms of the London Borough of Enfield granted in 1966.

Fig. 100   Egrentyne

Fig. 101   Enfield

Fig. 102   Heraldic antelope

Fig. 103   Heraldic ibex

Fig. 104   Heraldic tyger

HERALDIC ANTELOPE *(Fig. 102,* see also *Plate XV)* This curious creature has the body of a stag, the tail of a unicorn, the head of an heraldic tyger, a tusk or horn issuing from its nose and from its lower jaw, tufts of hair for a mane and two straight serrated horns. It is easily confused with the heraldic ibex. The antelope is mentioned by Spenser in *The Faerie Queene* as a wild beast, 'both fierce and fell'. The antelope was used as an heraldic badge by Henry V and can be seen on his tomb in Westminster Abbey. Also borne on the shield and crest of Snowe of Chicksands contained in the records of the College of Arms.

HERALDIC IBEX *(Fig. 103)* The creature is based upon the natural ibex but it has tusks, a small horn on the point of its nose and two long curved and serrated horns. These horns sweep over its back unlike the heraldic antelope's horns which point upwards. Apart from this slight distinction the two beasts seem to be identical.

HERALDIC PANTHER or PANTHER INCENSED (see *Plate XV)* In general appearance it is much like a leopard and always guardant issuing flames and smoke from its mouth and ears. Its body is usually covered with multi-coloured spots, the coat being white. The heraldic panther symbolizes aggression. Like all cats, this legendary beast literally spits fire. Some writers aver that the vapours were of a sweet nature, but it would seem likely that, like the bonacon, the fumes were emitted to cause distress to an adversary. The panther incensed is attributed as a badge to Henry VI, and is described as having fragrant breath 'that steameth forth of his nosethrills, and eares like Smoke, which our Paynters mistaking, corruptly doe make fire'. Robert Cooke, Clarenceux King of Arms, granted a crest and supporters to the Company of Dyers in 1577, to be added to the shield of arms already in use. The supporters were two panthers incensed proper, both ducally crowned Or. Heraldic panthers are also the supporters of the coat of arms of the Worshipful Company of Painter-Stainers; the coloured spots represent daubs of colour on the craftsman's smock.

HERALDIC TYGER (Tigris) *(Fig. 104,* see also *Plate XV)* A wolf-like beast with a tufted mane, tusks issuing from its mouth and a horn protruding from its nose, not to be confused with the natural or Bengal tiger. The heraldic tyger was attributed with 'dreadful swiftness' and remarkable ferocity. Its origins are in Asia where tiger meat is eaten to give strength and courage; eating the genitals supposedly promotes fertility.

Tyger cubs were, in legend, stolen for their various properties and the hunters were naturally pursued by the parent animals who wished to retrieve their young. To escape from the frenzied adult tygers, the hunters would throw down a looking glass in the path of the tygers who would gaze into the mirror, thinking that their reflection was their young one. The bewilderment of the parent animals gave the hunters time to effect their escape. The heraldic tyger is seen in the arms and crest of Thomas Sybell of Aynsford, Kent, entered in the Heralds' Visitation of that county in 1531. The blazon states: 'Argent a Tyger statant tail cowed Gules gazing at its reflection in a Hand-mirror erect frame and handle Or reflecting the head of a Tyger Gules'.

MALE GRIFFIN *(Fig. 105*, see also *Plate XIV)* The male griffin is similar to an ordinary griffin but without wings. Its body issues tufts of pointed rays or spikes and is probably a misrepresentation of a vulture with its feathers being lifted by the wind, combined with a lion. It is not so popular in heraldry as the ordinary griffin but still represents vigilance and strength. Both kinds of griffin have male attributes; there is no such creature as a female griffin.

MUSIMON (see *Plate XV)* A fictitious beast engendered by a goat and a ram, probably derived from the Moufflon wild sheep of southern Europe. It has the body of a goat with the head and horns of a ram and is also equipped with a pair of goat's horns. No example is known outside the Tudor heraldic textbooks.

NEBEK *(Fig. 106)* This is another small dog-like animal with a long tail and a wrinkled snout. The body is covered with tufts of hair. The nebek was the heraldic badge, and supporters, of Sir William Fitzwilliam, K.G., Earl of Southampton, and can be seen on his Garter stall-plate in St George's Chapel, Windsor.

PANTHEON *(Fig. 107)* This beast looks somewhat like a deer or an ass, having a solid body and long ears. It has cloven hooves and a bushy tail, and its body is always powdered with stars. A Tudor creation, the pantheon was granted to Henry Northey in 1556, and an earlier crest was granted in 1531 to Sir Christopher Baynham who bore a pantheon statant Sable powdered with gold estoiles, the ears and legs Gules. Pantheons are seen as supporters to the arms of the Marquess of Winchester.

Fig. 105   Male griffin

Fig. 106   Nebek

Fig. 107   Pantheon

Fig. 108   Parandrus

Fig. 109   Polyger

PARANDRUS *(Fig. 108)* The Cambridge Bestiary knew this beast but not many other authorities do. The creature apparently came from Ethiopia where it was known for its shaggy coat, the head of a stag, cloven hooves and branching horns. It was very timid and had the ability to change its colour according to its surroundings. The parandrus is seen in the records of the College of Arms supporting the heraldic banner of Sir Thomas Cheyney, K.G.

POLYGER *(Fig. 109)* A little-known creature, nevertheless recorded at the College of Arms, it seems to resemble a lion with horns of an antelope or yale. Although 'on record', it never seems to have been used.

TROGODICE *(Fig. 110)* This beast looks very much like a stag but its antlers sweep downwards and forwards like a reindeer. Granted to Robert Knyght, of Bromley, in 1549 by Thomas Hawley, Clarenceux King of Arms.

UNICORN (see *Plate XVI*) According to ancient legends this fabulous beast was a small, delicate but ferocious quadruped. It is usually depicted white with a gold horn, mane and tufts, referred to in heraldic blazon as 'armed, crined and unguled Or'. Its hooves are cleft and its horn has a barley-sugar twist which resembles the long tooth of the narwhal. Legend asserts that it could only be lured into captivity or killed by a pure virgin in whose lap the unicorn would lay its head, whereupon it was taken by the hunters. It is not known

Fig. 110   Trogodice

why the unicorn was hunted unless it was for the proverbial use of its single horn which apparently possessed singular virtues. When ground to a powder by the apothecaries of the day, it was used for healing purposes. The most famous unicorn appears of course as a supporter in the English and Scottish royal coat of arms. Unicorns also appear in the arms of the Worshipful Company of Apothecaries and in the arms of the Heraldry Society. The Wax Chandlers' Company has used unicorns as supporters since 1530.

YALE or EALE (see *Plate XV*) A buffalo-like beast possessing a pair of enormous curved horns which, according to legend, could rotate independently and constantly face an adversary. It also has tusks and a mane. Its origin was probably in India, where a water-buffalo, when roused, tends to fight by lunging with one horn unlike a domestic bull which butts with both horns. The yale is one of the Queen's Beasts, a set of heraldic animals created for the coronation of Her Majesty the Queen in 1953. The beast is seen holding a shield charged with the royal badge of a crowned portcullis, and a copy of the original set of beasts is on display in Kew Gardens, London. The yale may also be seen above the gateway to St John's College, Cambridge, which was founded by Lady Margaret Beaufort, and above the gateway of Christ's College which benefited from her estate. Also an heraldic supporter of the Dukes of Beaufort.

YPOTRYLL *(Fig. 111)* The badge of John Tiptoft, Earl of Worcester, is a very curious creature indeed. It looks like a camel with a boar's head complete with tusks, cloven hooves and a long smooth tail. The hairy humps on its back are shown in gold on a white skin in Fenn's *Book of Badges*.

Fig. 111   Ypotryll

a

b

Fig. 112
a Feathered angel with a rebec
b Cherubims

HUMANOID

CELESTIAL BEINGS *(Fig. 112, see also Plate XIV)* Generally clad in white flowing robes like an alb with a girdle and sometimes a scarf or amice, celestial beings are shown in human form with wings issuing from the back. Angels of different degrees and orders were given their own colours and precious stones. All degrees of angels have a nimbus or halo behind the head, either a plane disc of light or rays of gold similar to a glory. *Fig. 112 a* shows a fully-fledged crowned angel with a nimbus and playing on a rebec, from a fifteenth-century stained-glass window. Celestial beings such as angels are known in many cultures and religions. There are nine choirs of angels, each with its own chief. The choirs are divided into three orders: Cherubim, Seraphim and Thrones; Dominions, Virtues and Powers; and Principalities, Archangels and Angels. In ecclesiastical heraldry throughout the world and in several English families angels and cherubims are seen both as supporters and charges. The Child family has a cherubim, see *Fig. 112b*. Lord Meston has a standing angel crowned with an Eastern crown as his crest. The arms of the Abbey of St Albans are supported by two kneeling angels. The Worshipful Company of Fletchers in the City of London was granted a demi-angel as their crest in 1467, by William Hawkeslowe, Clarenceux King of Arms.

CENTAUR *(Fig. 113)* The centaur, see *Fig. 113a*, has the body of a horse combined with the torso, arms, head and shoulders of a man. The head is generally shown as bald and mischievous. Homer describes the centaurs as a wild mountain tribe of great ferocity but makes no mention of the horse or ox-like hind quarters, and it seems that the change took place later. The centaur is shown with a bended bow and is one of the twelve signs of the Zodiac where he is known as Sagittarius, see *Fig. 113b*. The battle of the centaurs is the best-known story about these mythical creatures. At the wedding of Pirithous and Hippodamia, a leading centaur, Eurytion, tried to carry off the bride which naturally led to a fight which the centaurs lost and were then banished from the country. Chiron the centaur is well known for instructing Achilles in the arts of music, medicine and hunting. Heracles accidentally wounded Chiron fatally with a poisoned arrow. The blazon for the crest of Lambart, Earls of Cavan is 'On a mount Vert, a Centaur proper drawing his bow Gules arrow Or'. The centaur also appears in the crests of Askelom, Bendlowes, Cromie, Cruell Petty and Petty-

Fitzmaurice. Sagittarius is the badge of an esquire, see *Fig. 113c*. The centaur, appropriate to those who are eminent in the field, is traditionally assigned to King Stephen and can be seen in the Palace of Westminster.

IPOTANE *(Fig. 114)* Mentioned by Sir John de Mandeville in 1499, it seems to be a curious monster, half man and half horse but without front legs. Mandeville says: 'In Bacharie ben many Ipotanes that dwellen sometimes in the water and sometimes on the land; and thei ben half man and half horse and thei eten men when thei may take him'.

Fig. 113a   Centaur

Fig. 114   Ipotane

Fig. 113b   Sagittarius

LAMIA or **EMIPUSA** *(Fig. 115)* A swift four-footed creature with the head and breasts of a young woman. An important note for identification is that the hindlegs have cloven hooves whereas the forelegs have claws. According to *Brewer's Dictionary of Phrase and Fable*, 'Lamia is a female phantom whose name was used by the Greeks and Romans as a

Fig. 115   Lamia

Fig. 113c   Sagittarius, the badge of an esquire

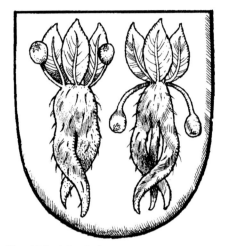

Fig. 116 Mandrake

Fig. 117 Manticora

Fig. 118 Satyr

bugbear to children, from the classic fable of a Lybian queen beloved by Jupiter, but robbed of her children by Juno; and in consequence she vowed vengeance against all children whom she delighted to entice and murder'.

MANDRAKE *(Fig. 116)* A plant, the root of which sometimes takes a human form both male and female. It is said to have aphrodisiac and narcotic properties and it was used as an anaesthetic in ancient Greece. If a mandrake plant is forcibly uprooted and pulled from the soil, it is said to shriek and the person who so violated it would die or become insane. One French family and one English family have the mandrake in their arms. Bodyam of Bodyam in Essex bear the arms: 'Gyronny of eight Gules and Sable three male demi-Mandrake Argent, the hair, leaves and apples Or, within a Bordure Or charged with eight Cross Crosslets fitchy Azure. And for the Crest upon a wreath Or and Azure a "shee Mandrake" Argent, the hair, leaves and apples proper, charged on the breast with a Cross Crosslet fitchy Sable'. These arms were confirmed between 1536 and 1547.

> . . . shrieks, like mandrakes torn out of the earth,
> That living mortals, hearing them, run mad.
>
> Shakespeare, *Romeo and Juliet*

MANTICORA, MANTIGER or SATYRAL *(Fig. 117)* The mantiger is another rare creature and a figment of the fecund imagination of early heralds, based no doubt upon the tales of long forgotten travellers. It has the shape of a lion complete with mane and claws but with the head of an old man displaying tusks and two long straight horns. The legend exists in a number of cultures that certain humans have the ability to transform themselves into animals, either at will or under the influence of some curse or spell. Werewolves fall into this category in Europe but in India it seems that the tiger rather than the wolf became the *alter ego*. The mantiger or manticora was well enough known for several writers to describe the beast. It had a triple row of teeth and a sting in its tail formed from sharp pointed quills. Its voice, we are told, was like a small trumpet. The mantiger is to be found in the arms of Lord Stawell and also in the arms of the Earls of Huntingdon.

SATYR *(Fig. 118)* This ithyphallic creature is of human form and usually naked, constantly reinforcing his reputation for lechery. His upper half is like a man but with long ears and short horns. His legs are like those of a goat with cloven hooves. Randle Holme confirms that the satyr had a sharp-pointed penis. The satyr's reputation is not good. Full of impishness and lechery, he seems constatnly to have been on the look-out for any opportunity. He is sometimes shown with wings (Merchant Adventurers of Bristol), but this is unusual. The satyr is associated with the rustic god Pan who, among other attributes, was a musician which may account for his appearance as a supporter to the now extinct Academy of the Muses. When the academy existed in the City of London, they bore for their dexter supporter a satyr, probably Pan.

THE SPHINX *(Fig. 119)* There are two kinds of sphinx, the Egyptian sphinx, see *Fig. 119a*, and the Greek sphinx, see *Fig. 119b*, and both are usually depicted couchant. The Egyptian sphinx has the body of a lion and the head is either that of a human, a ram or a hawk, and is always male. The Theban or Greek sphinx, see *Fig. 119c*, has the body of a lion with a human female head and breasts and wings issuing from its back. The Egyptian sphinx when shown with a human head wears a head-dress whereas the Greek sphinx always has flowing hair. The Egyptian sphinx was a religious symbol and was worshipped as a deity. Its attributes are associated with Osiris and Ammon, Neph and Helios. Physical power combined with wisdom and royal dignity seem to be its main features. Its other attributes are secrecy and religious mystery. The word *sphynx* in Chaldean means 'overflowing' which in itself is something of a mystery. The sphinx is used by British regiments which have connections with Egypt. It is the crest of the Asgill baronetcy, the Lambert and Goatly families and Sir John Moore.

Fig. 119a Egyptian sphinx

Fig. 119b Greek sphinx

Fig. 119c Standing Greek sphinx

WINGED

ALERION *(Fig. 120)* A small eagle usually shown displayed and without beak or legs. This creature is used in the arms of Lorraine, namely, 'Or on a bend Gules three alerions Argent'. The arms of Lorraine are said to commemorate an event when Godfrey de Boulogne shot three legless birds with one arrow. The House of Lorraine descends from Godfrey. The alerion is to be seen in the Chief of the armorial bearings of the city of Nancy where it is borne in pretence on the arms of the Dukes of Lorraine. The word alerion is an anagram of loraine which may be a clue to the origin of the name.

BASILISK (see Cockatrice, *Plate XIII*) Also called the amphysian cockatrice, the basilisk is exactly the same as a cockatrice with the addition of another head, a serpent's, at the end of its tail. Its breath and bite were deadly. In Christian art the little King of Serpents is the emblem of deadly sin, and the spirit of evil. Many writers through the ages have mentioned the basilisk, including Shakespeare, Dryden, Boswell, Pliny and others. Earl Howe has for his heraldic supporters two cockatrices (amphysian) wings elevated, the tails nowed, and ending in a serpent's head Or, combed, wattled and legged Gules. As the basilisk had such a monstrous reputation, even though it was only six inches long, it is difficult to understand why over twenty families in England have this creature in their arms.

COCKATRICE (see *Plate XIII)* The upper half of this monstrous creature is that of a cockerel, or wild red jungle-fowl with comb and wattles, while the lower half of the body is that of a serpent terminating in a barbed point. The two forelegs have the claws of a fighting cock, and from its back issue two bat-like wings (*Gallu gallus*). If it has a serpent's head at the end of its tail, it is known as a basilisk from the Greek word for king because of its triple-tufted crest which resembles a crown. It is said to have been hatched by a serpent from the egg of a cock. An alternative version states that these monsters were hatched by a toad from the egg of a dunghill cock, but as the creature is half cock and half serpent, the former origin seems more logical! There are references to the cockatrice in the Bible.

> And the sucking child shall play on the hole of the asp, and the weaned child shall put his hand on the cockatrice' den.

Fig. 120   Alerion

Isaiah, XI, 8

For Behold. I will send serpents, cockatrices, among you which shall not be charmed, and they shall bite you saith the Lord.

Jeremiah, VIII, 17

HARPY *(Fig. 121)* Depicted and described as a monstrous and filthy bird, half-woman and half-vulture. Its head and breast are generally shown as a human female conjoined to the body, its wings and tail that of a fierce and loathsome bird of prey. The Harpy is not a popular charge in English heraldry but there are one or two examples. In a church in Huntingdon there is a monument with a coat bearing Azure a Harpy with her wings disclosed, her hair flotant Or, armed of the same. The coat of arms of the city of Nuremburg has a Harpy; Azure a Harpy displayed armed, crined and crowned Or. This device appears as early as 1243. Richard III of England used a curious device based upon a Harpy – a falcon with the head of a maiden, holding the white rose of York.

Fig. 121 Harpy

> Of monsters all, most monstrous this; no greater wrath
> God sends 'mongst men; it comes from depth of pitchy
>   hell:
> And virgin's face, but womb like gulf unsatiate hath,
> Her hands are gripping claws, her colour pale and fell.
>   Virgil

HERALDIC PELICAN (see *Plate II)* Termed 'in her piety' and shown in her nest with young ones whom she is nourishing with her own blood. The mother bird is portrayed wounding, or vulning herself to feed her young. The young birds had been slain by serpents but the mother bird revived them with her blood. The legend must have originated from casual observers seeing the natural pelican feeding its young from the pouch beneath its bill and, as the tip of a pelican's beak is red, a mistaken idea was formed that it had wounded itself. The heraldic pelican looks more like an eagle than a pelican in nature. A number of churches use the pelican in her piety to support the lectern more usually held by an eagle. The arms of Corpus Christi College, Cambridge, show the pelican. The family of Chauntrell bears Gules a pelican in her piety Or. The family of Pelham from Somerset have Azure three pelicans Argent vulning themselves proper. Alphonso the Wise, King of Castile, used a pelican in the thirteeenth century. Pelicans are used as supporters by the Worshipful Company of Poulterers in the City of London. It is a symbol of charity and salvation, and of Christ who saved mankind by His Blood.

Fig. 122 Phoenix

Fig. 123 Tragopan

PHOENIX *(Fig. 122)* An imaginary bird resembling a pheasant of the Indian ornamental variety. Generally shown with wings displayed emerging from flames of fire. The legendary bird is said to have lived in North Africa for five hundred years and then, feeling weary, it flew with a host of other birds to Egypt where it built for itself a funeral pyre of wonderful spices and scented wood wherein it settled. The rays of the sun were so attracted to this marvellous sight that the tinder soon kindled and the phoenix was consumed by the fire. When the fire was out, some writers say that a grub-like insect emerged from the ashes and transformed itself into the new phoenix, others have written that the new bird arose from the flames which is certainly a more picturesque view. The phoenix represents resurrection and early monastic writers referred to Jesus Christ as the Phoenix. The Worshipful Company of Painter-Stainers in the City of London uses the phoenix in its arms and its crest to illustrate both their religious commitment and the fact that the phoenix is multicoloured, reflecting the gorgeous effect of the feathers of a pheasant and that of a painter's palette. The Blacksmiths' Company also uses the phoenix gazing at the sun, in its crest, the symbolism being that new things are created in the heat of the fire.

> . . . in Arabia there is one tree, the phoenix throne – one
> phoenix
> At this hour reigneth there.
>
> Shakespeare, *The Tempest*, Act III, Scene iii

TRAGOPAN *(Fig. 123)* An eagle with the horns of a ram. There is only one example of a tragopan in English heraldry. This curious bird was granted to Robert Lord by Clarenceux King of Arms Benolt and Garter King of Arms Wriothesley during the reign of Henry VIII. It is only seen in the College of Arms records and on personal items owned by the Lord family.

WINGED QUADRUPED

CATOBLEPAS *(Fig. 124)* A fictitious quadruped with a head so heavy that it always faced the ground which was fortunate as its gaze was fatal. Catoblepas is the genetic term for the gnu. It is mentioned by Pliny and used on one occasion in heraldry as a crest.

GAMELYON *(Fig. 125)* This creature has the body of a lion, the head and tail of a dog and the wings of a dragon. Invented by Sir William Dethick, Garter King of Arms, and granted to Thomas Gardner of South Brent in Devon, in 1557.

GRIFFIN or **GRYPHON** *(Fig. 126,* see also *Plate XIV)* The upper half of the body is that of an eagle with wings, forelegs, claws, ears and a beard. The lower half is the body of a lion with a tail. The origins of the griffin are very ancient probably coming from Egypt. The creature features in many cultures, especially in Asia and Africa, and later in Europe.

Fig. 125   Gamelyon

Fig. 124   Catoblepas

Fig. 126   Griffin

The griffin represents security and guardianship combined with vigilance. It is said to sleep with its eyes open.

HIPPOGRIF or **HIPPOGRYPH SIMOORGH** *(Fig. 127)* A winged horse whose father was a griffin and mother a filly, it has the head and forelegs of a griffin and the rear part of a horse. Not known in English heraldry.

> So saying he caught him up, and without wing
> Of hippogrif, bore through the air sublime
> Over the wilderness and o'er the plain.
>
> Milton, *Paradise Regained*

OPINICUS or **EPIMACUS** (see *Plate XIV)* This is another variation on the theme of the griffin. It has a lion's body and legs with claws, the head and wings of an eagle, with the tail of a camel. It does not appear to have the ears of a 'normal' griffin. It is sometimes seen without wings. The arms of the Worshipful Company of Barber Surgeons of London have for their heraldic supporters 'Two opinici Vert purfled Or, beaked Sable, wings Gules', and two of the same beasts support the armorial bearings of the Plasterer's Company. Another grant gives only the crest as an opinicus, with lynx as supporters.

Fig. 127   Hippogrif

PEGASUS *(Fig. 128*, see also *Plate XIV)* The winged horse of Greek mythology. It was caught by Bellerophon when it came down to drink at the spring of Pirene. Minerva assisted Bellerophon in placing a bridle on Pegasus. He then engaged the dreaded chimera and killed it with his arrows. Encouraged by his success, Bellerophon attempted to fly to the heavens on Pegasus but Zeus sent a gadfly to sting the horse and throw its rider. Pegasus continued his journey to the stables of Zeus. It could be argued that there is but one pegasus; however, the Merchant Adventurers were granted two as supporters to their arms, and even a third as their crest.

WINGED BULL *(Fig. 129*, see also *Plate XIV)* Depicted as an ordinary domestic bull with the wings of an eagle emanating from the shoulders. The wings, horns and hooves are often shown in gold. Mostly seen in ecclesiatical heraldry as the beast of St Luke. A grant of arms, crest and supporters to the Company of Butchers in 1540 describes the crest as a 'flying bull Argent, wings endorsed Or and Argent armed, crined and unguled Or, over the head a small circle of glory proper'. And for the supporters, 'Two flying bulls Argent, winged armed and unguled Or over each head a small circle of glory proper'.

Fig. 128   Pegasus

Fig. 129   Winged bull

Fig. 130   Amphisboena

Fig. 131   Dragon

REPTILIAN

AMPHISBOENA *(Fig. 130)* This monster is another serpent with wings, two legs and an additional head at the end of the tail. It was supposed to be very small, about the size of an earthworm. Towards the end of the fourteenth century most of the conventional beasts and monsters in heraldry had been overworked and it was deemed acceptable to employ such fabulous creatures as the Amphisboena.

> With complicated monsters' head and tail
> Scorpion and Asp and Amphisboena dire.
>
> Milton

AMPHITÈRE (see *Plate XIII*) A flying serpent with the wings of a dragon and a barbed tail, found in medieval bestiaries. The arms of the Portuguese poet Cameons are 'Azure an amphitère Or, rising between two mountains Argent'.

DRAGON *(Fig. 131*, see also *Plate XIII)* A reptilian winged quadruped with a scaly body and a barbed tongue. The tail is also barbed and a horn is shown on its nose. It has strong claws and long bat-like ears. The dragon appears in the legends and mythology of many cultures. Russia and Britain share the legend of St George and the Dragon. Germany has the '*Lintworm*' which was especially favoured by the composer Wagner. China has its own kind of dragon, a cousin of the European monster, which is to be found in heraldry accredited to persons and organizations of Oriental origin. The dragon is the royal device and national symbol of Wales, and features as supporters of the arms of the City of London.

HYDRA (see *Plate XIII*) A dragon with seven heads ultimately slain by Hercules. One of the twelve labours of Hercules was to kill the Lernean hydra which was laying waste to the marshes it inhabited, killing both men and beasts. It is generally shown with conventional dragon's heads at the end of long necks issuing from the body, which has four legs with claws and wings. The tail terminates in a barbed point. This is not a popular monster but it can be seen in the arms of Crespine and Downes, and the family of Barret of Avely in Essex have the Hydra as their crest, namely; 'A Hydra, wings endorsed Vert, scaled Or'.

> Seven great heads out of his body grew,
> An iron breast, and back of scaly brass;
> And all imbrued in blood his eyes did shine as glass,
> His tail was stretched out in wondrous length.
>
> Spenser, *The Faerie Queene*, Book I, c.vii

SALAMANDER *(Fig. 132)* A mythical venomous reptile generally portrayed as a lizard or newt reclining upon a bed of fire. Its back is usually shown bedight of stars. Origins in Egypt and used as a royal French badge.

SERPENT-WOMAN *(Fig. 133*, see also *Plate XIV)* A monster sometimes used to decorate ancient manuscripts but not seen in any specific coats of arms.

WYVERN (see *Plate XIII)* The upper part of the body is similar to a dragon with bat-like wings, two forelegs with strong claws and long ears. The lower half of the body is that of a coiled serpent with its tail terminating in a barbed point. A device that may be recognized on the flags in the Bayeux tapestry. It was used by the kings of Wessex and is now displayed by a regiment in the British army. The Worshipful Company of Weavers, in the City of London, was granted two wyverns as supporters to its arms in 1616, by Sir William Segar, Clarenceux King of Arms. They had borne arms since their first grant in 1490 but without supporters.

Fig. 133 Serpent-woman

Fig. 132 Salamander

Fig. 134   Cock-fish

MER-CREATURES

COCK-FISH *(Fig. 134)* The upper half is a farmyard cockerel with comb and wattles with his wings displayed and the lower half is that of a fish. Any number of these half-fish exist but there are some like the sea-dog which does not have a tail, but webbed paws and a fin. Used in European heraldry.

MERMAID and MELUSINE *(Fig. 135)* The upper half of a mermaid's body is that of a human female shown nude, while the lower half is that of a fish with fins and a tail. She is usually depicted with long hair and holding a mirror in her right hand and a comb in her left. The mermaid, see *Fig. 135b*, appears in the mythology of many cultures and must have been created from seafarers' tales. The dugong or seacow, a walrus-like creature, is often quoted as the origin of the mermaid. Fake mermaids were made in the nineteenth century for fairs and showgrounds, by joining the body of half a dried monkey to the tail of a dried fish. A mermaid with two tails is called a melusine, see *Fig. 135a* and *c*, which is seen in Germany more often than in England. There is also one example of a mermaid with three tails but her name is unknown.

Fig. 135a   Melusine

Fig. 135b   Mermaid

From Greek mythology to Wagner, water females have always been associated with temptation and treachery. The mermaid's reputation is so bad that it makes one wonder why anyone should want to represent her but she is part of maritime legend and is good-looking. Over thirty-six English families, however, bear a mermaid in their arms or their crest, and many corporate bodies connected with the sea also make use of this creature. The Worshipful Company of Fishmongers has a mermaid as a supporter and the Merchant Adventurers of Bristol used a mermaid holding an anchor. The Austrian family of Estenburger bears the unusual crest of a mermaid without arms, but having wings. Well-known mermaid crests belong to the families of Ellis, Mason, Balfour of Burleigh, and Wallop, Earls of Portsmouth. The mermaid has been used as a badge in addition to her use in arms and crests. The monumental brass (1392) of Lord Berkeley, at Wooton-under-Edge, shows Lord Berkeley wearing a collar of mermaids over his camail.

Fig. 135c   Melusine

NEPTUNE or POSEIDON *(Fig. 136)* The sea-god Neptune or Poseidon (Greek name) is shown as an elderly but sturdy and virile man with flowing locks and a full beard. To denote his sovereignty, he wears an Eastern crown and toga-like raiment secured around his waist with a cord or a scarf. In his hand he holds a trident. Edmund Spenser's words 'First came great Neptune with his three-forked mace' may reflect that Oar Maces of Admiralty have been used as symbols of legal authority since the reign of Elizabeth I. Poseidon was the sea-god of the ancient Greeks, and it was to him they made sacrifices for safe journeys and safe deliverance. He is often depicted in the company of other sea deities, dolphins and sea-horses. In the arms of Lord Hawke, Admiral and Commander-in-Chief of the Fleet, Vice-Admiral of Great Britain, 1776, the dexter supporter is a figure of Neptune, his mantle Vert edged Argent, crowned with an Eastern crown Or, his dexter arm erect and holding a trident pointing downwards in the act of striking Sable, headed Argent, and resting his left foot on a dolphin proper. Sir Isaac Heard, Garter King of Arms, bore Neptune as the principal charge in his arms.

Fig. 136   Neptune

TRITON *(Fig. 137)* Triton was the son of Neptune and Amphitrite, half man and half fish so a merman. Always shown with a beard and a head-band on his flowing hair, holding a trident and a conch shell horn. His appearance is very similar to his father, but without crown. Some writers assumed that a race of mermen sprang from Triton, all of

Fig. 137   Triton

whom were referred to as 'a Triton'. Much used by sea-faring men and organizations with maritime connections. The City of Liverpool has a Triton or merman for its sinister supporter. Lord Lyttelton has two mermen for his supporters. The Fishmongers' Company in the City of London was granted supporters in 1575, when they were described as 'A Merman his upper partes armed his nether part of a fyshe, all naturall, in his right hand holdinge a faucheron and with his left susteyninge the Heaulme and Tymbre: And on the left syde of the sayde Armes a Mermayde with her right hand supporting the Armes and in her lefte bearinge a mirrour or looking glasse all in proper colour'.

Tritons were also used in Tudor and Elizabethan times by the Royal Fishery Company, the Academy of Muses which boasted a merman with two tails (see Melusine, page 102) and the Bermudas (or Summer Islands) Company.

> Triton, who boasts his high Neptunian race
> Sprung from the God by Salace's embrace.
>
> Camoens, *Lusiad*

> Triton his trumpet shrill before them blew
> For goodly triumph and great joliment
> That made the rocks to roar as they were rent.
>
> Spenser, *The Faerie Queene*

GLOSSARY OF TERMS

A.   Sometimes used as an abbreviation of 'Argent' in trick (*vide*).

Abatement   A mark for illegitimacy or disgrace. Nine exist and must be in Sanguine or Tenné colours. Seldom used in practice.

Abeyance   The state of a peerage when it cannot be claimed properly by two or more claimants who have equal rights.

à bouche   The notch or lance rest in the corner of a shield. From the French for mouth.

Achievement   A complete coat of arms with shield, helm, wreath, crest, mantling and usually a motto.

Addorsed   Term used when two animals are shown back to back.

Adumbration   Artistic shading to make the charges on a shield appear to stand out.

Affronté   Facing the front (looking out of the shield at the spectator).

Ailettes   Square protective plates worn on the shoulders by early knights to guard the neck. Often painted with arms. From the French for a type of wing.

Allusive arms   Coats of arms relating to an office, not the holder.

Anchor   An anchor has a beam, a shaft and flukes which may be a different colour. It may be plain or fouled by a cable or chain.

Annulet   A small ring.

Antique crown   A crown with five triangular points rising from the rim.

Apaumé   A hand erect showing the palm.

Arblast   A crossbow.

Argent   Silver, usually shown as white.

Armed   Term used to denote the claws, talons and horns of beasts when a different colour from the body.

Armiger   One who is entitled to a coat of arms.

Armory   The subject of armorial bearings. A record of families and coats of arms.

Arms   Abbreviation for coat of arms. Heraldic devices were embroidered or painted onto coats or tabards, hence the name.

At gaze   When a stag is standing but facing out of the shield.

Attainder   Removal by law of all rights and privileges.

Attires   The antlers of a stag.

Augmentations   Additions to a coat of arms as a reward and mark of honour.

Azure   The heraldic word for blue (az. or b.) from the Arabic *lazura*.

Badge   An adjunct to a coat of arms usually borne by retainers.

Balance   A pair of scales.

Banner   A square flag displaying personal arms.

Bar   A horizontal stripe taking up about one-fifth of the area of the shield.

Barb   The sepals of an heraldic rose, usually shown as green; also the head of an arrow.

Baron   The lowest rank in the peerage of Great Britain.

Baronet   An hereditary knight ranking below the peerage.

Barrulet   The diminutive of a bar.

Barry   A shield divided horizontally into a number of specified stripes.

Base   The lower portion of a shield.

Baton   A couped cotise, or a couped bendlet, the ends of which do not reach the sides of the shield. Also an alternative word for a wand of office.

Bearing   As in armorial bearings. Any item that appears on an heraldic shield.

Bedight   Arranged or adorned.

Belt and buckle   Often used in Scotland to encircle a clan crest.

Bend   A diagonal stripe from the dexter chief to the sinister base, i.e. from the top left-hand corner to the lower right-hand corner. The width is about one-fifth of the width of the shield when it appears undecorated but slightly wider when it is charged.

Bendlet   The diminutive of and thinner than a bend.

Bezant   A gold disc, often used to suggest money.

Bi-corporate   Used for an animal with one head but two bodies.

Blazon   Heraldic jargon used to describe any piece of armory.

Bluemantle   An English Officer of Arms. He is a Pursuivant which is the lowest of the three ranks of officers in the College of Heralds. The office is said to have been instituted by Henry V to perform heraldic duties for the Order of the Garter in the mid-fifteenth century.

Boar's head   Originally known as sanglier. Shown either erased (torn off) or couped (cut close).

Bonnet   The red velvet cap lined with ermine that appears within the coronets of peers of the realm. See also Cap of Estate.

Bordure   A border running round the perimeter of the shield.

Botonny cross   A cross with the ends of the arms terminating in three balls.

Bouget   Two animal bladders on a yoke used for carrying water. Sometimes referred to as a water-bouget.

Bow   Usually of three loops and known as a true-love's knot, seen at the top of spinsters' lozenges.

Brass   An etched metal plate usually placed in the floor of a church as a memorial to a knight or a prelate.

Broad arrow   This is a large arrowhead or spearhead like a pheon but without the engrailed inner edges of the point.

Brock   A badger.

Caboshed   A word used to describe the head of an animal, which is usually a stag, cut off close behind the ears and facing out of the shield. No part of the neck is visible.

Cadency   The system of placing a small mark on a shield to indicate the relationship with the head of the family, i.e. first son, second son, etc. Nine symbols are generally shown in the reference books. Daughters do not use cadency marks.

Caduceus   The staff or wand of Mercury, messenger of the gods, often used in heraldic designs to suggest speed, communication and efficiency.

Cannon   Usually shown as an artillery piece rather than a naval gun.

Canting arms   A visual pun or play upon a name or occupation.

Canton   A square shape in the chief of the shield slightly smaller in size than a quarter.

Caparisoned   A description of a warhorse with harness, saddle-cloth, armour and bedight with heraldry.

Cap of Estate or Cap of Maintenance   Sometimes called a chapeau, it is usually red turned up ermine with the rim terminating in a point. It is the kind of headgear that actors wear when playing the part of Robin Hood.

Carrick Pursuivant   A Scottish officer of arms.

Cat-a-mountain   A wild highland cat.

Celestial crown   A crown with five triangular points rising from the rim, each point having a star at the tip.

Cercele   A type of cross with two almost circular hoops at the ends of the arms.

Chamfron   Armour for a horse's head.

Chape   The metal tip at the end of a sword scabbard.

Charge   Any item illustrated on a shield on one or both sides of an ordinary.

Charger   A large circular metal plate.

Checky   An area divided into squares like a chess board.

Cherub   A child's head between a pair of opened wings.

Chessrook   The chess piece known as the rook (from the Italian *rocca*, meaning a tower or castle) is in the form of a tower in the game, but looks rather different in heraldry, having two curved points at the top.

Chevron   A gable-like member rising to a point above the centre of the shield. It is an ordinary and should occupy about one-fifth of the shield.

Chief   The first of the ordinaries, a horizontal stripe taking up slightly less than one-third of the shield from the top downwards.

Cinquefoil   A floral form having five leaves. It is sometimes pierced in the centre.

Clarenceux King of Arms   The second most senior Herald in England.

Civic crown   A circlet or wreath of oak leaves and acorns.

Clarion or rest   A well-known device whose origins are lost in the mists of time. It has been suggested that it is a portable organ or a spear-rest or even a ship's rudder.

Climant   Term used for a goat rampant.

Cognizance   Visual identification especially of an heraldic nature.

Cointise   Obsolete word for mantling.

Collars   Gold chains of office and the highest ranks of orders of chivalry.

Combatant   When two animals are rampant and facing each other, this term is used. They should appear to be fighting.

Combed   This refer to the comb of a cock.

Compartment   When a coat of arms has supporters, they must stand on a compartment which is usually a mound of grass, sometimes scattered with flowers or other appropriate objects. Water is to be seen where the supporters are ships.

Complement   When a full moon is shown on a shield, the moon is said to be 'in her complement'.

Compony   A single row of squares or rectangles such as one would see on the edge of a flag. Also known as gobony.

Confronté   Similar to combatant. Animals facing each other but not fighting.

Conjoined   Joined together.

Contourné   The same as regardant. Facing to the sinister.

Cony   The old name for a rabbit.

Cork Herald   Formerly an Irish Herald.

Coronet   A minor crown granted to peers of the realm and only worn at coronations.

Cotise   A thin line following the shape of an ordinary on its outer edge.

Couchant   Term for an animal lying down.

Counter   If a shield and an ordinarty are divided and the colours are alternate, then it is referred to as counterchanged.

Counter-embattled   Crenellations on both sides of an ordinary.

Couped   Cut short.

Courant   Running.

Coward   An animal with its tail between its legs.

Crenellated   Decorated with embrasures and merlons like the top of a tower or castle wall.

Crescent   Cadency mark for the second son.

Crest   The three-dimensional device fixed to the top of the helm which was a target in jousting. It is an important part of a coat of arms and can be used in isolation, for example on signet rings, motor-car doors and table silver.

Crest coronet   A gold rim with three strawberry leaves rising from it. Sometimes used instead of a crest wreath. It implies no rank precedence.

Crined   Term used for a mane or tufts of hair.

Cronel   The crown-shaped knob at the end of a tilting lance.

Crosier   The staff of a bishop or an abbot, shaped like a shepherd's crook.

Cross   The principal emblem of Christianity. Numerous varieties exist.

Crown   The symbol of sovereignty. The Crown Jewels at the Tower of London contain several examples including St Edward's Crown and the Imperial State Crown.

Crusily   Scattered with small crosses.

Cubit arm   An arm and hand, cut off below the elbow.

Cypher   A monogram often ensigned with a crown.

Dancetty A zigzag partition with fewer but bolder points than indented. A fess dancetty will probably have only three upward points.

Debruised A term used when a charge is laid over by an ordinary.

Decorations Insignia, medals and orders of chivalry sometimes shown on their ribbons beneath a shield of arms.

Decrescent A crescent with its horns to the sinister.

Degrees The steps, usually three in number, leading up to a Calvary cross. Sometimes known as grieces.

Demi The upper half of any item especially animal crests.

Devisal Not to be confused with device, which is another word for an heraldic badge. A devisal is a design of armorial bearings for certain countries where the British Crown has no authority. Permission from the foreign government must be obtained before the devisal can be authorized. When it is produced it does not have the British royal coat of arms on its heading.

Dexter The right-hand side of the shield as seen from behind.

Diaper An artistic technique decorating the surface of the shield and anything on it with low-key non-heraldic floral designs to enrich the general appearance.

Differencing To include in the heraldic design some difference from similar arms to denote cadency, illegitimacy, adoption or divorce.

Dimidiation The method of conjoining two shields by dividing them vertically and placing the outer halves together to form a single shield. Thus any ordinary or charge is only half visible and fixed to half of the charge on the other shield. More popular in Europe than in England.

Dingwall A Scottish Pursuivant of Arms.

Disarmed A creature without claws, teeth or horns.

Displayed A description of birds with their wings spread wide open.

Distilling Shedding drops, usually of blood.

Dormant Sleeping.

Doubled A word for the lining of a robe or the mantling in a coat of arms.

Dovetailed A partition line that resembles a dovetailed joint in cabinet-making.

Dublin Herald A former officer of arms in Ireland.

Ducal coronet The same as a crest coronet which has three strawberry leaves, and not to be confused with the coronet of a duke, which has five leaves.

Earl A rank in the peerage of Great Britain above Viscount and below Marquess.

Earl Marshal The hereditary office of the Dukes of Norfolk. The Great Officer of State responsible for ceremonial and head of the College of Arms.

Eastern crown A gold rim with five triangular points rising from it.

Electoral bonnet The ceremonial and state headgear used by the rulers of Hanover. It was portrayed in the British royal arms 1801–1816, after which Hanover became a kingdom and the bonnet was replaced by a crown.

Elevated Describing the wings of birds when raised.

Embattled An outline like the top of a castle wall with embrasures and merlons.

Emblazoning Describing a coat of arms in technical heraldic jargon.

Embowed Bent, as seen in a human elbow.

Embrued or imbrued Stained with blood.

Enfiled Encircled by a rim such as an annulet or a coronet.

Engrailed   A word used to describe the edge of an ordinary which has a continuous series of small semi-circular scallops rather like a saw blade.

Enhanced   Above its normal position.

Ensign   A type of flag used by the armed services. Ensigns also relate to a complete set of heraldic achievements including badges and standards.

Ensigned   The term used when describing a shield with a crown above it, i.e. ensigned by the royal crown.

En soleil   A charge issuing rays of the sun.

Environed   Surrounded

Eradicated   A tree or plant pulled out of the ground by its roots.

Erased   Torn off. Many crests have an animal's head erased, leaving three tufts of hair.

Escallop or scallop   A shell.

Escutcheon   An heraldic shield.

Esquire   The rank above a gentleman and below a knight. There were several grades of esquire through which a potential knight had to pass during his training.

Fasces   An axe contained in a bundle of rods bound with ribbons.

Fer-de-moline   A mill-rind, which was the metal centre of a mill-stone placed there to prevent the wearing down of the stone upon its driving shaft.

Fess   A horizontal stripe running across the shield and taking up approximately one-fifth of its area.

Fetterlock   A padlock which looks like an ancient 'D'-lock.

Field   The surface of an heraldic shield.

Fimbriated   A very thin outline of a different colour around an ordinary.

Fitchy   Term used when the lower arm of a cross has been sharpened to a point.

Fitzalan   An English officer of arms known as a Pursuivant Extraordinary. This means that he does not practice daily at the College of Arms.

Flambeau   A flaming torch, not to be confused with beacon or cresset.

Fleury or flory   A term used when an ordinary or a field is decorated with fleur-de-lys.

Flighted   Term which can be used instead of fletched when describing the colour of the feathers on an arrow.

Flittermouse   A bat.

Flukes   The blades at the ends of an anchor.

Fly   The part of a flag furthest away from the flag-pole.

Forcene   The word used for a rearing horse which would be described as rampant if it were a lion.

Fountain   A roundel that is barry-wavy Argent and Azure.

Fret   A geometric design with a lozenge-shaped square interlaced with two batons in saltire.

Fructed   A tree or plant bearing fruit.

Fusil   A narrow lozenge.

Fylfot   The swastika.

Gamb   The leg of a beast.

Garb   A wheatsheaf, from the French *gerbe*.

Garnished   The decorative parts of an item are so described when in a different colour.

Garter   A circular strap with a buckle, usually edged with gold and with the end of the garter looped behind the buckle and hanging down vertically.

Garter King of Arms   The senior King of Arms in England responsible to the Earl Marshal for the running of the College of Arms and many official duties.

Ged   A pike fish.

Gemelles   Two barrulets close together and always used in pairs.

Gentleman   The armorial and social rank above yeoman and below esquire. To bear arms lawfully qualifies a man to the title of gentleman.

Glory   A halo.

Gobony   The same as compony.

Golpe   A purple roundel.

Gonfanon   A long flag suspended from an horizontal pole. Much used by Tudor sailors between the masts of their vessels.

Gorges   An heraldic representation of a whirlpool.

Goutte   A drop of liquid.

Grant of Arms   A document signed and sealed by the Kings of Arms in the form of Letters Patent, by direction of the Earl Marshal, granting new arms, crest and sometimes a badge to a petitioner. An hereditary honour from the crown.

Grieces   The three steps leading up to a Calvary Cross, also known as degrees.

Gringolé   Decorated with the heads of serpents.

Guardant   The term used when a beast or monster has its face turned towards the viewer.

Guidon   A type of flag.

Gules   The colour red, from the Arabic *gul* a red rose.

Gun-stone   A black roundel, presumably a cannon-ball.

Gyron   The lower half of a quarter or a canton when divided from dexter chief to sinister base. A wedge shape.

Habited   Clothed.

Harp   Stringed musical instrument depicted either as an Irish harp or as a female angel with her wings forming the upper beam of the instrument.

Hart   A male (red) deer after its fifth year.

Hatchment   A lozenge-shaped funeral painting of a coat of arms on a black background denoting the decease of an armiger.

Hauriant   A fish shown in a vertical position with head upwards.

Hawk   The general term for a bird of prey used in falconry.

Heiress   A daughter of an armiger with no living brothers.

Helm   Protective armour for the head and used in heraldry to denote rank.

Herald   The general term for an officer of arms of any rank.

Hind   A deer shown with no antlers.

Hoist   The part of a flag closest to the flag-pole.

Honorary arms   Coats of arms granted to foreign nationals on condition that they can prove their descent from a subject of the British Crown and place a pedigree on record at the College of Arms.

Humetty   Cut short at the ends.

Hurst   A small plantation of trees, i.e. Coneyhurst means the wood where rabbits live.

Hurt   A blue roundel. A bruise.

Imbrued   See embrued.

Impaled   Two coats of arms occupying the two sides of a shield divided vertically down the centre. The method of displaying the arms of a man and his wife, or a person and his office.

Imperial Crown   A representation of the royal crown with semi-circular arches.

Incensed   Having the appearance of fire issuing from the mouth and ears.

Increscent   A crescent having its horns to the dexter.

Indented   A zigzag, sawtoothed outline to any ordinary.

Infulae   The ribbons hanging down from a mitre.

Insignia   Any badge, collar, wand or decoration relating particularly to an official office or an order of chivalry.

Invected   The opposite of engrailed, i.e. having continuous cusps connected in a partition line or on the outer edge of an ordinary.

Irradiated   Issuing rays of the sun, generally shown as pointed straight and wavy alternately.

Issuant   Emerging from.

Jelloped   The wattles of a cockerel.

Jessant   Spouting forth.

Jupon   A close-fitting sleeveless tunic with a scalloped hem.

Key   The position of the wards (fretted blades at the end of the key) must be described.

King of Arms   The rank of the three senior heralds: Garter King of Arms, Clarenceux King of Arms (with jurisdiction south of the River Trent) and Norroy & Ulster King of Arms (with jurisdiction north of the River Trent up to the Scottish border, and Northern Ireland). The orders of chivalry also have Kings of Arms but their duties are of a non-heraldic nature.

Knight   The ancient rank of Christian chivalry allowing the holder to use the prefix 'Sir' before his name, or 'Dame' if the recipient is female.

Knot   A decorative interlaced design based upon cords and ribbons. There are many different knots in heraldry.

Knowed   Knotted.

Label   A mark of cadency for the eldest son within his father's lifetime. A horizontal strip with three points or tongues attached to it vertically. There may be more points and they may be charged with some small items of heraldry to differentiate members of a large family such as the royal family.

Lady   The official title of the wife of a knight, baronet or baron. The title 'Lady' is used as a prefix to her Christian name only when she is a daughter of an earl, marquess or duke.

Lambrequin   The mantling attached to the helm and used in a decorative manner at the sides of the shield.

Lancaster Herald   An English Officer of Arms.

Langued   The word used when referring to the tongue of a beast.

Lined   Refers to the lining of the mantling.

Lists   A tournament area.

Liver-bird   A cormorant or shag.

Livery colours   The colours adopted by a family for its retainers, and used in the mantling and wreath of the coat of arms. The colours are usually based on the principal colour and metal of the shield.

Lodged   A term used for stags, etc. when at rest.

Long cross   A plain cross with the central member considerably longer than the horizontal beam.

Lozenge   A diamond-shaped charge. The shape of 'shield' used for women and for funeral hatchments.

Luce   A pike fish.

Lymphad   An ancient galley shown with or without oars and sails.

Lyon King of Arms   The senior herald in Scotland. The Court of Lord Lyon King of Arms is the Scottish equivalent to the English College of Arms but has different rules and regulations.

Mace   A symbol of authority.

Main   A hand.

Maltese Cross   A cross of eight points, the arms being triangular, each terminating in two points.

Man   Isle of Man. Formerly a kingdom, now under the jurisdiction of Norroy & Ulster King of Arms.

Mantle   The robe of a peer of the realm.

Mantling   The decorative fabric covering of an heraldic helm. It was used to protect the metal from the sun and rain, and is now used in heraldry to embellish the sides of a coat of arms, hanging down from the wreath.

Marchmont Herald   A Scottish officer of arms.

Marquess   A peer of the realm, above an earl and below a duke.

Marshal   Marshal of England is one of the titles held by the Duke of Norfolk as the hereditary Earl Marshal.

Martel   A hammer.

Martlet   A swallow or swift shown without feet, the legs being covered by two tufts of feathers. The cadency mark of a fourth son.

Mascle   A voided lozenge. The mark of a divorced woman.

Masoned   The word used to describe the cement between the brickwork of towers, etc. when showing a different colour from the bricks.

Matriculation   The Scottish system whereby the sons of an armiger must have their armorial bearings confirmed by Lord Lyon with their own marks of cadency.

Maunch   A long sleeve from a woman's dress.

Medal   A metal decoration, usually circular, suspended from a coloured ribbon. Originally awarded for acts of distinction by the Honourable East India Company, and privately before the custom was adopted by the British government.

Melusine   A mermaid with two tails.

Membered   The legs and beak of a bird.

Merchants' marks   Non-heraldic symbols used by guilds of merchants to identify their work.

Mercury   Messenger of the gods.

Metals   In heraldry the metals are gold and silver (Or and Argent).

Mill-rind   See Fer-de-moline. The metal centre of a millstone.

Mitre   The tall headgear of a bishop.

Moline cross   A cross which has its ends terminating in two curved points.

Monogram   A decorative use of intertwined letters.

Moor   Usually just the head of a coloured man with curly hair.

Motto   The legend or war-cry that appears on a scroll beneath the shield in a coat of arms. It does not officially form part of the armorial bearings and can be omitted or changed at will. Any language may be used.

Mound   The orb. A symbol of sovereignty, being the world surmounted by a cross. Of great Christian significance.

Mount   A small hill usually covered with grass.

Mural crown   A rim with its upper edge crenellated and bricks indicated. See Masoned.

Murrey   A dark red tincture like the mulberry.

Naiant   Swimming.

Navel point   A position on the shield in the centre and below the middle.

Nebuly   A partition line that is formed from nodules like a jigsaw-puzzle piece. From the French *nébuleux*, meaning cloudy. It is often used as the outline of ordinaries.

Nimbus   A halo.

Nombril point   The same as navel point of a shield.

Norroy King of Arms   The third most senior herald in England with jurisdiction north of the River Trent up to the Scottish border.

Officers of arms   Heralds.

Ogress   A black disc.

Oppressed   One charge lying upon another.

Or   The metal gold.

Orb   The mound. A gold ball surmounted by a cross supported by straps on the upper hemisphere. A symbol of Christian authority.

Order   Orders of Chivalry are: The Most Noble Order of the Garter; The Most Honourable Order of the Bath; The Most Distinguished Order of Saint Michael and Saint George; The Royal Victorian Order and The Most Excellent Order of the British Empire; The Most Ancient and Most Noble Order of the Thistle. There are several other Orders such as St Patrick and St John but the Indian Empire Orders are falling into disuse as their members decline.

Ordinary   The principal dividing members of a shield, i.e. bar, bend, chevron, fess, etc.

Ordinary of Arms   A book containing descriptions of coats of arms classified according to their principal charges.

Organ-rest   A clarion. The origin of this is uncertain, possibly a portable organ.

Orle   A narrow border within the shield following the contours of the curve.

Ostrich feathers   Three ostrich feathers issuing from a coronet form the badge of the Prince of Wales.

Over all   This literally means that a charge is laid directly on top of another.

Padlock   The word 'pad' is associated with the foot and padlocks, like fetter-locks, were originally used to secure the ankles of prisoners.

Pairle   A 'Y'-shaped division of the shield.

Pale   A vertical stripe about one-fifth of the width of the shield, hence palings in a fence.

Palisado crown   See Vallary crown. A circlet set with seven vertical pieces pointed at the top and riveted to the rim.

Pall   A 'Y'-shaped figure conjoining the three points of the shield.

Pallet   The diminutive of a pale.

Palmer's staff   A pilgrim's walking stick with a decorative head.

Paly   Any number of thin vertical stripes on the shield. The number should however be specified.

Panache   A pyramidal bunch of feathers used in ancient crests.

Papal crown   A tall conical hat enfiled by three coronets and surmounted by an orb.

Party or parted   A vertical division where one side is a different colour to the other.

Partition lines   Invisible lines of division within a shield determining the areas for different colours. These outlines are not necessarily straight and may be engrailed, invected, wavy, nebuly, indented, dancetty, embattled, raguly, dovetailed, potenty, angled, bevelled, escartelly, nowy, embattled grady, enarched, urdy and rayonné.

Pascuant   Grazing.

Passant   Term for a quadruped standing on three legs with the right foreleg raised. The beast can also be Passant guardant, i.e. looking out at the observer, or Passant regardant, which indicates that the beast is looking back over its shoulder.

Passion   Passion-cross and Passion-nails are representations of the instruments of the crucifixion of Jesus Christ.

Patonce cross   This is a broader version of the cross flory.

Paty   The description of a cross with splayed ends.

Peacock   Blazoned as 'in his pride' when its tail feathers are displayed.

Pearl   The word used for the silver balls set upon the rim of some coronets of peers of the realm.

Peer   A member of the peerage, i.e. Baron, Viscount, Earl, Marquess, Duke.

Pellet   A black roundel otherwise called a gunstone.

Pendent   Hanging below or beneath.

Pennon   A long streamer flag.

Per   A preposition meaning 'by', hence per chevron, per fess, etc., to indicate the general division of the shield by partition lines.

Pierced   Any charge pierced with a hole so that the colour of the shield shows through it.

Pile   A wedge-shaped ordinary that issues from the chief. It can however be a pile reversed, that is issuing from the base of the shield or even from the flanks of the shield. From the Latin *pilum*, meaning a javelin; it presumably alludes to the point.

Pinioned   Having wings.

Plate   A silver roundel or dish.

Plenitude   The word used when the moon is shown as a full moon.

Plume   A long feather or feathers.

Poix   Black spots of liquid rather than ermine spots. Goutté de poix.

Pomme cross   A cross with the ends terminating in a round pommel like the pommel on the hilt of a sword.

Pomme Pomeis   A green roundel. An apple.

Pommel   The ball or knot at the end of a sword hilt. Sometimes decorated with a shield of arms.

Popinjay   A parrot.

Port   The gate of a castle. There are old terms for the position of the portcullis but these are rarely, if ever, used now.

Portcullis Pursuivant   An English officer of arms whose office was established by Henry VII, in 1499. An officer in ordinary, on daily duty at the College of Arms.

Potent   One of the furs used in heraldry. Potent looks like a capital 'T' and is the ancient word for a crutch.

Potenty   A partition line made up from alternating 'T'-shapes.

ppr   The abbreviation for proper, meaning any item shown in its natural colours.

Pretence   A shield shown in pretence means that it is displayed in the centre of another shield. A man who marries an heraldic heiress places her arms on a small shield in the centre of his own as he pretends to the estates of her family, there being no male heirs. After the death of the mother, her children can quarter their paternal arms with those of their mother.

Preying   Used when one beast or monster is preying upon another.

Priests   The Clerks in Holy Orders of most churches have their own insignia indicating their position in the ecclesiastical hierarchy.

Proboscis   An elephant's trunk. Sometimes used in European heraldry as part of a crest. More often two trunks are used which look like horns.

Pronominal arms   The paternal coat in quartered arms.

Purfled   A term, also used in violin-making, meaning a thin line of decoration or plain running round the inside edge of any item.

Purpure   Purple, abbreviated to 'purp'.

Pursuivant   From the French to pursue; the lowest rank of officers of arms. The titles are Portcullis, Rouge Dragon, Rouge Croix and Bluemantle.

Quadrate   Square.

Quarter   One-fourth division of a shield, in cross.

Quarterings   Arms which are placed together upon one shield to indicate family relationships. Any number can be used, but the more quarterings that are used, the less direct the design becomes.

Quatrefoil   A four-leaved heraldic device.

Queue   The tail of an animal.

Quill   A goose-feather stripped and trimmed for writing. Usually shown unstripped and recognizable as a feather. Calligraphers trim them down to a slender spike.

Quise   Taken off at the thigh.

Rabbit   Known as a cony.

Ragged (staff)   Having the smaller branches cut off but leaving the stumps.

Raguly   A partition line made up from diagonal stumps.

Rampant   The description of a beast such as a lion leaping but with its left rear foot still on the ground. The left foreleg is shown in a lower position to the right one.

Rayonné   Issuing rays of light.

Rebated   Cut-off.

Rebus   A non-heraldic visual pun upon a name. Commonly used where a craftsman was not entitled to arms but wished to be recorded in a light-hearted manner.

Recercelé   Curled.

Reflexed   Carried backwards, as in a lion with its tail reflexed over the back.

Regardant   Term for an animal when looking backwards.

Respectant   Animals when face to face.

Rising   A bird about to take off.

Rod of Aesculapius   A snake entwined around a staff. A symbol of healing.

Rolls of Arms   Long strips of vellum painted with shields of arms and rolled up rather than cut into pages and bound as a book. The earliest records in the College of Arms are in this form.

Rompu   Broken.

Rothesay Herald   A Scottish officer of arms.

Rouge Dragon Pursuivant   An English Officer of Arms.

Rouge Croix Pursuivant   An English herald, whose office was established in 1418. Named after the red cross of St George.

Roundel   A circular disc, of various colours. Each coloured roundel has its own name.

Rowel   The star-shaped wheel of a spur.

Rustre   A narrow lozenge pierced with a circular hole.

Sable   The colour or tincture black, named after the small animal with a black coat. Abbreviated to 'sa' in heraldry.

Salient   An animal leaping or reaching up with both its hindlegs on the ground and both its forelegs stretching upwards.

Saltire   A St Andrew's cross with the beams extending from the upper corners of the shield down to the lower flanks.

Sang   Blood.

Sanglier   A wild boar.

Sanguine   A blood-red colour.

Sans   The French term for 'without'.

Savage   Generally seen as a Green Man or Man of the Woods, having oak-leaves wreathed about his temples and loins and holding a club. See also Wild man.

Saxon crown   An ancient and simple form of crown with three pearls raised on points from the rim. Ribbons or infulae and bells are sometimes seen on early coins and seals.

Scaling ladder   A broad ladder, equipped with hooks at the top, for scaling castle walls.

Scallop   See Escallop.

Scrip   A pilgrim's pouch or wallet.

Scroll   See Motto.

Seal   A wax impression taken from a matrix containing arms, crest motto and decorations. Used for identifying the signatory of a document or for sealing letters before envelopes came into common use. The Great Seal of the United Kingdom is used for crown documents and Letters Patent.

Seax   A curve-bladed, notched scimitar.

Segreant   A rampant griffin with its wings together.

Sejant   The sitting position.

Semé   Scattered with or strewn with.

Shafted   The handle of a spear or the length of an arrow.

Shakefork   A pall with the ends couped.

Shamrock   The emblem of Ireland.

Shield   The centrepiece of a coat of arms. Formerly a portable piece of armour usually carried on the left arm in combat.

Sinister   The left-hand side of a shield as seen by the person holding it, and the right-hand side as seen by an observer.

Sinople   The word in French heraldry for green.

Siren   A mermaid.

Slip   A twig pulled off the branch, generally shown with two leaves.

Somerset Herald   An English officer of arms.

Stains   Tenné or tawny, Sanguine or blood red and Murrey or mulberry.

Stall-plate   A metal plate enamelled with the arms of a knight and placed above his stall in the chapel of his order of chivalry.

Standard   A long flag displaying arms in the hoist, with crest and badge in the fly separated by two stripes bearing a motto. The standard is tapered down to a semi-circular or swallowtailed end.

Star   Always shown as a five-pointed mullet with straight points, or as an estoille with wavy points, unless otherwise stated in the blazon.

Statant   Standing.

Stock   The stump of a tree or the shaft of an anchor.

Sun   The sun is described in heraldry as 'in splendour' and it is shown with a human face.

Sunburst   Pointed and wavy gold rays issuing from a cloud.

Supporters   Beasts or monsters and even human beings on either side of the shield in a coat of arms supporting the shield. They are granted only to peers of the realm, knights grand cross of the orders of chivalry and corporate bodies. Exceptions do exist but the general rule is to keep supporters exclusively for the peerage and highest ranks of knighthood.

Swastika   Known in heraldry as a fylfot.

Tabard   The garment of an herald bearing arms. It has a flat front and back with two sleeveless sides attached by ribbons. It is worn over Royal Household uniform and only in the presence of the sovereign. In former times, Pursuivants wore tabards that were shorter at the front and back.

Talbot   A large dog akin to a bloodhound.

Targe   A small round shield.

Tau cross   A 'T'-shaped cross, which does not cross.

Tenné   Tawney.

Thistle   The Order of the Thistle is the principal order of chivalry in Scotland. The thistle flower is a royal badge.

Thunderbolt   The symbol and weapon of Zeus. The thunderbolt is represented as a cigar-shaped central rod issuing zigzag flashes of lightening between two displayed wings.

Tierced   Divided into three pieces.

Tinctures   Colours.

Torque   An heraldic wreath, also torse.

Torteau   A red roundel.

Tournament   A sporting combat between knights on horseback, organized with very strict rules.

Trefoil   An heraldic flower with three leaves, usually slipped, meaning that there is a stalk.

Tressure   A thin border running round the inner edge of the shield, as seen in the royal arms of Scotland where there is a double tressure flory-counter-flory. It is in fact a diminutive of the orle.

Trian aspect   The term indicates that the crest and helm are set at such an angle that the observer can see part of the reverse side, i.e. three-quarter view.

Trick; Tricking   The method of indicating colours of a coat of arms by means of abbreviated words on a black and white drawing.

Tricorporate   A fabulous beast with three bodies conjoined to one head. Usually drawn on a shield so that the head is in the centre with the bodies pointing towards the three corners of the shield.

Trident   Neptune's three-tined spear.

Trippant   The description of a stag when passant.

Triton   A minor sea-god shown in the shape of a merman. Supposed to be the son of Poseidon and Amphitrite. Often portrayed with a conch-shell horn and a trident. A merman is generally described as a triton.

Trussed   A bird with the wings closed.

Trussing   A bird of prey devouring another.

Tun   A barrel.

Tynes   The points on the antlers or attires of a stag.

Ulster King of Arms   The principal officer of arms for Northern Ireland. The office is now held by Norroy King of Arms, hence his title Norroy & Ulster.

Undy   Another word for a wavy line.

Unguled   The word for the hooves of animals when a different colour from the body.

Unicorn Pursuivant   A Scottish officer of arms.

Union flag   The national flag of Great Britain comprising the crosses of St George, St Andrew and St Patrick. Often incorrectly called the Union Jack because it is flown from the Jack staff in a warship.

Urchin   A hedgehog.

Urdy cross   A cross with lozenge-shaped ends.

Uriant   The term used when a fish on a shield is diving downwards.

Vair   One of the furs in heraldry. It is made up from small shield-shaped pieces and is blue and white unless described otherwise.

Vallary crown   A crown similar to a Palisado crown but with five visible pointed pales rising from the rim.

Vert   Green.

Vested   Clothed.

Virolles   The metal ferrules binding a hunting-horn. They may be a different colour to the horn.

Viscount   The peerage rank above baron and below earl.

Voided   Having the centre taken out.

Volant   Flying.

Vulned   Wounded.

Wales   The Prince of Wales is always the eldest son of the sovereign. There is an officer of arms called Wales Herald of Arms Extraordinary, whose duties are purely ceremonial. This office was created in 1963.

Wand   A staff of office.

Water   Usually depicted as barry wavy Argent and Azure.

Water-bouget   Two animal-skin bags or bladders suspended from a yoke, for carrying water. Used as a charge in heraldry.

Wattled   This refers to the wattles of a cock, and not a fence.

Wavy   An undulating line.

Weel   A basket device for catching fish.

Wheatsheaf   Known as a garb.

Wheel   Usually a cartwheel or Catherine wheel with spikes issuing from the rim, but occasionally a cogwheel.

Whirlpool   A spiral device starting from the centre of the shield and extending to its extremities.

White Ensign   The flag of the Royal Navy. It is a white flag with the red cross of St George throughout and the Union in the first quarter.

Widow's cordon   This is seldom, if ever, used now, but a widow may place a knotted rope or cordon around the arms of her deceased husband upon a lozenge.

Wild man   A wodehouse or savage. A recluse who lived in the forest and dressed in animal skins and wreaths of vegetation. Usually depicted holding a cudgel and sometimes with his knees and elbows visible through his rustic garb. He appears in English and Continental heraldry and in church architecture.

Windsor Herald   An English Officer of Arms.

Wings   These are generally shown displayed unless blazoned otherwise.

Winnowing fans   In appearance similar to flat baskets and used to blow the chaff from the grain. The best-known example is to be seen in the monumental brass of Sir Robert de Setvans where the fans appear on his shield, his surcoat and his ailettes (*c.* 1305).

Wreath   Sometimes called a 'torse', the wreath is a circlet of twisted fabric obscuring the joint and the laces securing the crest to the helm. It is usually depicted in six twists using the principal metal and tincture from the arms. The metal always comes first. When drawing a crest, the wreath must be shown to avoid confusion with an heraldic badge which does not have a wreath.

York Herald   An English officer of arms. The office was probably instituted in 1484 but it could have been earlier. Now an officer in ordinary on daily duty at the College of Arms.

Yoke   The horizontal beam from which hang water-bougets.

ORGANIZATIONS AND ASSOCIATIONS

The College of Arms
Queen Victoria Street
London EC4V 4BT

Founded in 1484, the College of Arms is the central body for organizing and recording everything armorial in England. It is part of the royal household and deals with ceremonial and research enquiries on a daily basis. Each officer of arms has an ancient title attached to his office and supports the staff in his chambers with the contributions from fee-paying clients. The Duke of Norfolk as Earl Marshal is the head of the College and is responsible only to the sovereign. The thirteen officers are divided into ranks: three Kings of Arms, six Heralds and four Pursuivants.

The Heraldry Society
45 Museum Street
London WC1A 1LY

Founded in 1947 with members worldwide, the Heraldry Society is an amateur association for heraldic enthusiasts. It arranges lectures, outings and exhibitions.

The Society of Heraldic Arts
c/o The Hon. Secretary
46 Reigate Road
Reigate
Surrey RH2 0QN

The Society, founded in 1987, has both professional craft members and associate members. It exists to provide a network for heraldic artists and craftsmen.

Fig. 138 The College of Arms

SELECT BIBLIOGRAPHY

AND SUGGESTED FURTHER READING

Ashmole, Elias, *The Institution, Laws & Ceremonies of the most Noble Order of the Garter*, printed by F. Maycock for Nathaniel Brooke, at the Angel in Cornhill, 1692.

Barber, Richard and Riches, A., *A Dictionary of Fabulous Beasts*, Macmillan, 1971.

Baty, Thomas, *Vital Heraldry*, The Armorial, 1962.

Boutell, Rev. Charles, *Heraldry*, revised edition by J.P. Brooke-Little, Clarenceux King of Arms, Frederick Warne & Co. Ltd, 1970.

Burke, Sir Bernard, *Burke's General Armory*, Harrison, 1884.

Burke's Landed Gentry, Shaw Publishing Co. Ltd in conjunction with the Burke Publishing Co. Ltd, 1937.

Burns, Lt Cdr K.V., *Badges and Battle Honours of H.M. Ships*, Maritime Books, 1986.

Child, Heather and Colles, Dorothy, *Christian Symbols, Ancient and Modern*, Bell & Hyman, 1971.

Cole, Herbert, *Heraldry Decoration and Floral Forms*, Bracken Books, 1988.

Cussans, John E., *The Handbook of Heraldry*, 1868.

Dennys, Rodney and Quondam Somerset Herald, *The Heraldic Imagination*, Barrie & Jenkins, 1975.

Dorling, Rev. E.E., *Heraldry of the Church*, A.R. Mowbray & Co. Ltd, 1911.

Elvin, Charles Norton, *A Dictionary of Heraldry*, Kent & Co. Ltd, 1889.

Fairbairn, James, *Fairbairn's Crests of the Families of Great Britain and Ireland*, New Orchard Editions, 1986.

Ferguson, George, *Signs and Symbols in Christian Art*, A. Zwemmer Ltd, 1954.

Friar, Stephen, *A New Dictionary of Heraldry*, A. & C. Black, 1987.

Fox-Davies, *The Art of Heraldry*, 1909, republished Bloomsbury Books, 1986. *Complete Guide to Heraldry*, T.C. & E.C. Jack, 1909.

Garai, Jana, *The Book of Symbols*, Lorrimer Publishing, 1973.

Grant, Michael and Hazel, John, *Who's Who in Classical Mythology*, Weidenfeld & Nicholson, 1973.

Graves, Robert (introduction), *New Larousse Encyclopedia of Mythology*, Hamlyn Publishing Group, 1959.

Hall, Angus, *Monsters and Mythic Beasts*, Aldus Books, Jupiter Books, 1975.

Hasler, Charles, *The Royal Arms*, Jupiter Books, 1980.

Hope, Sir W.H. St John, *Heraldry for Craftsmen and Designers*, John Hogg, 1913.

Larkin, David, ed., *Faeries*, Pan Books, 1978.

Mann, Sir James, *European Arms and Armour*, published by the Trustees of the Wallace Collection under Crown Copyright, 1962.

Maxwell, W. Sterling, *Examples of the Ornamental Heraldry of the Sixteenth Century*, privately printed by Stephen Ayling, 1867.

Moir, Prebendary A.L., *The World Map in Hereford Cathedral*, Hereford Cathedral, 1975.

National Maritime Museum, Greenwich, London, *Oar Maces of Admiralty*, H.M. Stationery Office, 1966.

Neubecker, Ottfried, *Heraldry, Sources, Symbols and Meaning*, Macdonald & Jane's, 1977.

Papworth, John Woody, *Papworth's Ordinary of British Armorials*, reprinted from 1874 edition, Tabard Publications Ltd, 1961.

Parker, James, *A Glossary of Terms used in Heraldry*, James Parker & Co., 1894.

Pine, L.G., *International Heraldry*, David & Charles, 1970.

Rosignoli, Guido, *The Illustrated Encyclopaedia of Military Insignia of the Twentieth Century*, Chartwell Books Inc., 1986.

Saville, Margaret, *Royal Heritage*, Pitkin, 1953.

Smith, Whitney, *Flags and Arms Across the World*, Cassell, 1980.

Villiers, Elizabeth, *The Book of Charms* (first published as *The Mascot Book* in 1923), Lorrimer Publishing, 1973.

Vinycomb, John, *Fictitious and Symbolic Creatures in Art with special reference to their use in Heraldry*, Chapman & Hall Ltd, 1906.

Volborth, Carl-Alexander von, *The Art of Heraldry*, Blandford Press, 1987.

Wagner, Sir Anthony, *Heralds of England*, H.M. Stationery Office, 1967.

Welch, Charles, *Coat-Armour of the London Livery Companies*, privately printed, 1914.

Wilkinson-Latham, Robert, *Phaidon Guide to Antique Weapons and Armour*, Phaidon, 1981.

Woodford, James, *Heraldic Sculpture*, The Boydell Press, 1972.

INDEX

Note: Any words not found in the index may be found in the Glossary. Italic page numbers refer to line drawings; bold figures refer to plate numbers and their captions.